In Pursuit of Flavor

Tips and Tricks to Fry, Grill, Roast, and Bake

Linda D. Parker

Dinner for 12 persons.

First Course.—Soup à la Jardinière; chicken soup; crimped salmon and parsley-and-butter; trout aux fines herbes, in cases. *Entrées.*—Tendrons de veau and peas; lamb cutlets and cucumbers. *Second Course.*—Loin of veal à la Béchamel; roast fore-quarter of lamb; salad; braised ham, garnished with broad beans; vegetables. *Third Course.*—Roast ducks; turkey poult; stewed peas à la Française; lobster salad; cherry tart; raspberry-and-currant tart; custards, in glasses; lemon creams; Nesselrode pudding; marrow pudding. Dessert and ices.

Dinner for 8 persons.

First Course.—Green-pea soup; salmon and lobster sauce; crimped perch and Dutch sauce. *Entrées.*—Stewed veal and peas; lamb cutlets and cucumbers. *Second Course.*—Haunch of venison; boiled fowls à la Béchamel; braised ham; vegetables. *Third Course.*—Roast ducks; peas à la Française; lobster salad; strawberry cream; blancmange; cherry tart; cheesecakes; iced pudding. Dessert and ices.

Dinner for 6 persons.

First Course.—Soup à la Jardinière; salmon trout and parsley-and-butter; fillets of mackerel à la maître d'hôtel. *Entrées.*—Lobster cutlets; beef palates, à la Italienne. *Second Course.*—Roast lamb; boiled capon and white sauce; boiled tongue, garnished with small vegetable marrows; bacon and beans. *ThirdCourse.* —Goslings; whipped strawberry cream; raspberry-and-currant tart; meringues; cherry tartlets; iced pudding. Dessert and ices.

First Course.—Julienne soup; crimped salmon and caper sauce; whitebait. *Entrées.*—Croquettes à la Reine; curried lobster. *Second Course.*—Roast lamb; rump of beef à la Jardinière. *Third Course.*—Larded turkey poult; raspberry cream; cherry tart; custards, in glasses; Gâteaux à la Genévése; Nesselrode pudding. Dessert.

JULY,PlainFamilyDinnersfor .

Sunday.—1. Salmon trout and parsley-and-butter. 2. Roast fillet of veal, boiled bacon-cheek, peas, potatoes. 3. Raspberry-and-currant tart, baked custard pudding.

Monday.—1. Green-pea soup. 2. Roast fowls garnished with water-cresses; gravy, bread sauce; cold veal and salad. 3. Cherry tart.

Tuesday.—1. John dory and lobster sauce. 2. Curried fowl with remains of cold fowls, dish of rice, veal rolls with remains of cold fillet. 3. Strawberry cream.

Wednesday.—1. Roast leg of mutton, vegetable marrow and potatoes, melted butter. 2. Black-currant pudding.

Thursday.—1. Fried soles, anchovy sauce. 2. Mutton cutlets and tomato sauce, hashed mutton, peas, potatoes, 3. Lemon dumplings.

Friday.—1. Boiled brisket of beef, carrots, turnips, suet dumplings, peas, potatoes. 2. Baked semolina pudding.

Saturday.—1. Cold beef and salad, lamb cutlets and peas. 2. Rolled jam pudding.

Sunday.—1. Julienne soup. 2. Roast lamb, half calf's head, tongue and brains, boiled ham, peas and potatoes. 3. Cherry tart, custards.

Monday.—1. Hashed calf's head, cold lamb and salad. 2. Vegetable marrow and white sauce, instead of pudding.

Tuesday.—1. Stewed veal, with peas, young carrots, and potatoes. Small meat pie. 2. Raspberry-and-currant pudding.

Wednesday.—1. Roast ducks stuffed, gravy, peas, and potatoes; the remains of stewed veal rechauffé. 2. Macaroni served as a sweet pudding.

Thursday.—1. Slices of salmon and caper sauce. 2. Boiled knuckle of veal, parsley-and-butter, vegetable marrow and potatoes. 3. Black-currant pudding.

Friday.—1. Roast shoulder of mutton, onion sauce, peas and potatoes. 2. Cherry tart, baked custard pudding.

Saturday.—1. Minced mutton, rump-steak-and-kidney pudding. 2. Baked lemon pudding.

JULY, Things in Season.

Fish.—Carp, crayfish, dory, flounders, haddocks, herrings, lobsters, mackerel, mullet, pike, plaice, prawns, salmon, shrimps, soles, sturgeon, tench, thornback.

Meat.—Beef, lamb, mutton, veal, buck venison.

Poultry.—Chickens, ducklings, fowls, green geese, leverets, plovers, pullets, rabbits, turkey poults, wheatears, wild ducks (called flappers).

Vegetables.—Artichokes, asparagus, beans, cabbages, carrots, cauliflowers, celery, cresses, endive, lettuces, mushrooms, onions, peas, radishes, small salading, sea-kale, sprouts, turnips, vegetable marrow,— various herbs.

Fruit.—Apricots, cherries, currants, figs, gooseberries, melons, nectarines, pears, pineapples, plums, raspberries, strawberries, walnuts in high season, for pickling.

JULIENNE, Soup à la.

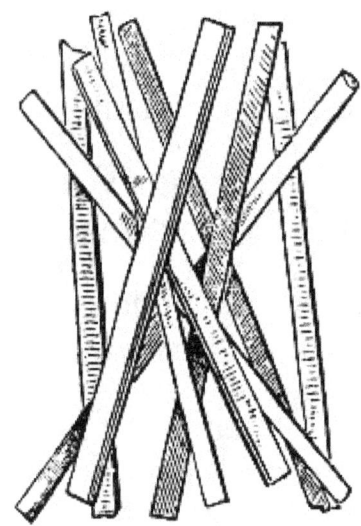

STRIPS OF VEGETABLE.

Ingredients.—½ pint of carrots, ½ pint of turnips, ¼ pint of onions, 2 or 3 leeks, ½ head of celery, 1 lettuce, a little sorrel and chervil, if liked, 2 oz. of butter, 2 quarts of stock. *Mode.*—Cut the vegetables into strips of about 1¼ inch long, and be particular they are all the same size, or some will be hard whilst the others will be done to a pulp. Cut the lettuce, sorrel, and chervil into larger pieces; fry the carrots in the butter, and pour the stock boiling to them. When this is done, add all the other vegetables and herbs, and stew gently for at least an hour. Skim off all the fat, pour the soup over thin slices of bread, cut round about the size of a shilling, and serve. *Time.*—1½ hour. *Average cost.*—1s. 3d. per quart. *Seasonable* all the year. *Sufficient* for 8 persons.

Note.—In summer, green peas, asparagus-tops, French beans, &c., can be added. When the vegetables are very strong, instead of frying them in butter at first, they should be blanched, and afterwards simmered in the stock.

KALE BROSE (a Scotch Recipe).

Ingredients.—Half an ox-head or cow-heel, a teacupful of toasted oatmeal, salt to taste, 2 handfuls of greens, 3 quarts of water. *Mode.*—Make a broth of the ox-head or cow-heel, and boil it till oil floats on the top of the liquor, then boil the greens, shred, in it. Put the oatmeal, with a little salt, into a basin, and mix with it quickly a teacupful of the fat broth: it should not run into one doughy mass, but form knots. Stir it into the whole, give one boil, and serve very hot. *Time.*—4 hours. *Average cost,* 8*d.* per quart. *Seasonable* all the year, but more suitable in winter. *Sufficient* for 10 persons.

KEGEREE.

Ingredients.—Any cold fish, 1 teacupful of boiled rice, 1 oz. of butter, 1 teaspoonful of mustard, 2 soft-boiled eggs, salt and cayenne to taste. *Mode.*—Pick the fish carefully from the bones, mix with the other ingredients, and serve very hot. The quantities may be varied according to the amount of fish used. *Time.*—¼ hour after the rice is boiled. *Averagecost* , 5*d.* exclusive of the fish.

KIDNEYS, Br oiled (aBr eakfastorSupperDish).

Ingredients.—Sheep kidneys, pepper and salt to taste. *Mode.*—Ascertain that the kidneys are fresh, and cut them open, very evenly, lengthwise, down to the root, for should one half be thicker than the other, one would be underdone whilst the other would be dried, but do not separate them; skin them, and pass a skewer under the white part of each half to keep them flat, and broil over a nice clear fire, placing the inside downwards; turn them when done enough on one side, and cook them on the other. Remove the skewers, place the kidneys on a very hot dish, season with pepper and salt, and put a tiny piece of butter in the middle of each; serve very hot and quickly, and send very hot plates to table. *Time.*—6 to 8 minutes. *Average cost,* 1½*d.* each. *Sufficient.*—Allow 1 for each person. *Seasonable* at any time.

KIDNEYS.

Note.—A prettier dish than the above may be made by serving the kidneys each on a piece of buttered toast cut in any fanciful shape. In this case a little lemon-juice will be found an improvement.

KIDNEYS, Fried.

Ingredients.—Kidneys, butter, pepper, and salt to taste. *Mode.*—Cut the kidneys open without quite dividing them, remove the skin, and put a small piece of butter in the frying-pan. When the butter is melted, lay in the kidneys the flat side downwards, and fry them for 7 or 8 minutes, turning them when they are half done. Serve on a piece of dry toast, season with pepper and salt, and put a small piece of butter in each kidney; pour the gravy from the pan over them, and serve very hot. *Time.*—7 or 8 minutes. *Average cost*, 1½d. each. *Sufficient.*—Allow 1 kidney to each person. *Seasonable* at any time.

KIDNEY OMELET (a favourite French Dish).

Ingredients.—6 eggs, 1 saltspoonful of salt, ½ saltspoonful of pepper, 2 sheep's kidneys, or 2 tablespoonfuls of minced veal kidney, 5 oz. of butter. *Mode.*—Skin the kidneys, cut them into small dice, and toss them in a frying-pan, in 1 oz. of butter, over the fire for 2 or 3 minutes. Mix the ingredients for the omelet, and when the eggs are well whisked, stir in the pieces of kidney. Make the butter hot in the frying-pan, and when it bubbles, pour in the omelet, and fry it over a gentle fire from 4 to 6 minutes. When the eggs are set, fold the edges over, so that the omelet assumes an oval form, and be careful that it is not too much done: to brown the top, hold the pan before the fire for a minute or two, or use a salamander until the desired colour is obtained, but never turn an omelet in the pan. Slip it carefully on to a *very hot* dish, or, what is a much safer method, put a dish on the omelet, and turn the pan quickly over. It should be served the instant it comes from the fire. *Time.*—4 to 6 minutes. *Average cost*, 1s. *Sufficient* for 4 persons. *Seasonable* at any time.

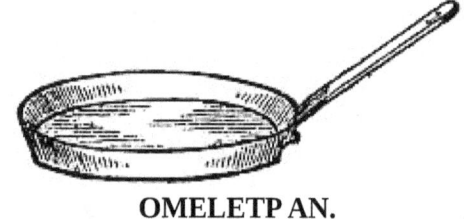

OMELET PAN.

KIDNEYS, Stewed.

Ingredients.—About 8 kidneys, a large dessertspoonful of chopped herbs, 2 oz. butter, 1 dessertspoonful of flour, a little gravy, juice of half a lemon, a teaspoonful of Harvey sauce and mushroom ketchup, cayenne, and salt to taste. *Mode.*—Strew the herbs, with cayenne and salt, over the kidneys, melt the butter in the frying-pan, put in the kidneys, and brown them nicely all round; when nearly done, stir in the flour, and shake them well; now add the gravy and sauce, and stew them for a few minutes, then turn them out into a dish garnished with fried sippets. *Time.*—10 or 12 minutes. *Seasonable* at any time.

LAMB.

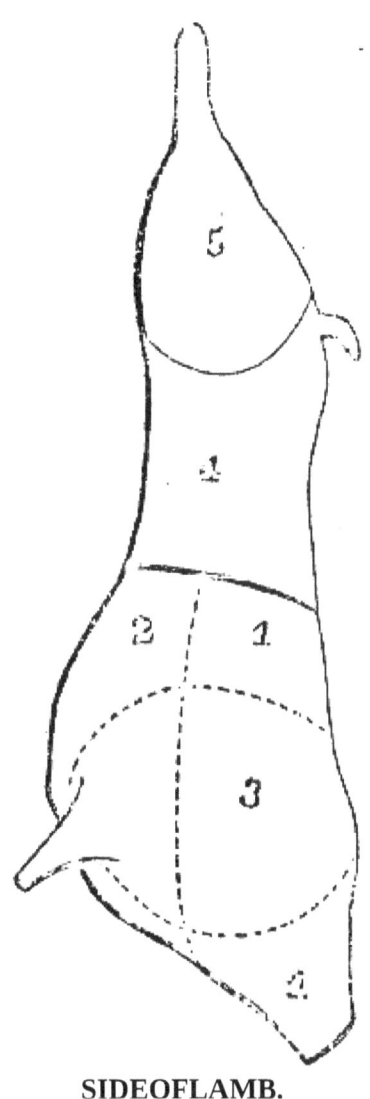

SIDE OF LAMB.

The most delicious sorts of lamb are those of the South-Down breed, known by their black feet; and of these, those which have been exclusively suckled on the milk of the parent ewe, are considered the finest. Next to these in estimation are those fed on the milk of several dams; and last of all, though the fattest, the grass-fed lamb: this, however, implies an age much greater than either of the others.

LAMB, in the early part of the season, however reared, is in London, and indeed generally, sold in quarters, divided with eleven ribs to the fore-quarter; but, as the season advances, these are subdivided into two, and the hind-quarter in the same manner; the first consisting of the shoulder, and the neck and breast; the latter, of the leg and the loin.—As lamb, from the juicy nature of its flesh, is especially liable to spoil in unfavourable weather, it should be frequently wiped, so as to remove any moisture that may form on it.

IN THE PURCHASING OF LAMB FOR THE TABLE, there are certain signs by which the experienced judgment is able to form an accurate opinion whether the animal has been lately slaughtered, and whether the joints possess that condition of fibre indicative of good and wholesome meat. The first of these doubts may be solved satisfactorily by the bright and dilated appearance of the eye; the quality of the fore-quarter can always be guaranteed by the blue or healthy ruddiness of the jugular, or vein of the neck; while the rigidity of the knuckle, and the firm, compact feel of the kidney, will answer in an equally positive manner for the integrity of the hind-quarter.

MODE OF CUTTING UP A SIDE OF LAMB IN LONDON.—1. Ribs; 2. Breast; 3. Shoulder; 4. Loin; 5. Leg; 1, 2, 3. Fore Quarter.

LAMB, Breast of, and Green Peas.

Ingredients.—1 breast of lamb, a few slices of bacon, ½ pint of stock, 1 lemon, 1 onion, 1 bunch of savoury herbs, green-peas. *Mode.*—Remove the skin from a breast of lamb, put it into a saucepan of boiling water, and let it simmer for 5 minutes. Take it out and lay it in cold water. Line the bottom of a stewpan with a few thin slices of bacon; lay the lamb on these; peel the lemon, cut it into slices, and put these on the meat, to keep it white and make it tender; cover with 1 or 2 more slices of bacon; add the stock, onion, and herbs, and set it on a slow fire to simmer very gently until tender. Have ready some green peas, put these on a dish, and place the lamb on the top of them. The appearance of this dish may be much improved by glazing the lamb, and spinach may be substituted for the peas when variety is desired. *Time.*—1½ hour. *Average cost*, 10*d.* per lb. *Sufficient* for 3 persons. *Seasonable.*—Grass lamb, from Easter to Michaelmas.

LAMB, Stewed Breast of.

Ingredients.—1 breast of lamb, pepper and salt to taste, sufficient stock to cover it, 1 glass of sherry, thickening of butter and flour. *Mode.*—Skin the lamb, cut it into pieces, and season them with pepper and salt; lay these in a stewpan, pour in sufficient stock or gravy to cover them, and stew very gently until tender, which will be in about 1½ hour. Just before serving, thicken the sauce with a little butter and flour; add the sherry, give one boil, and pour it over the meat. Green peas, or stewed mushrooms, may be strewed over the meat, and will be found a very great improvement. *Time.*—1½ hour. *Average cost*, 10*d.* per lb. *Sufficient* for 3 persons. *Seasonable.*—Grass lamb, from Easter to Michaelmas.

Lamb, to Carve.—Leg, loin, saddle, shoulder, are carved as mutton.

LAMB, Fore-quarter of, to Carve.

We always think that a good and practised carver delights in the manipulation of this joint, for there is a little field for his judgment and dexterity which does not always occur. The separation of the shoulder from the breast is the first point to be attended to; this is done by passing the knife round the dotted line, as shown by the figures 1, 2, 3, 4, and 5, so as to cut through the skin, and then, by raising with a little force the shoulder, into which the fork should be firmly fixed, it will come away with just a little more exercise of the knife. In dividing the shoulder and breast, the carver should take care not to cut away too much of the meat from the latter, as that would rather spoil its appearance when the shoulder is removed. The breast and shoulder being separated, it is usual to lay a small piece of butter, and sprinkle a little cayenne, lemon-juice, and salt between them; and when this is melted and incorporated with the meat and gravy, the shoulder may, as more convenient, be removed into another dish. The next operation is to separate the ribs from the brisket, by cutting through the meat on the line 5 to 6. The joint is then ready to be served to the guests; the ribs being carved in the direction of the lines from 9 to 10, and the brisket from 7 to 8. The carver should ask those at the table what parts they prefer —ribs, brisket, or a piece of the shoulder.

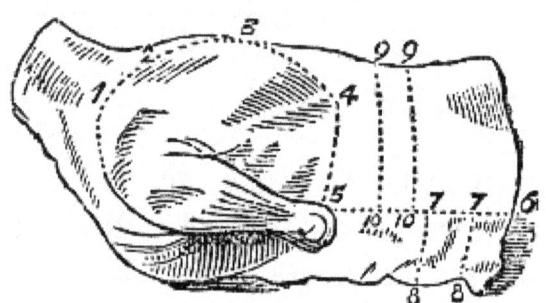

FORE-QUARTEROFLAMB.

LAMBCUTLETS.

Ingredients.—Loin of lamb, pepper and salt to taste. *Mode.*—Trim off the flap from a fine loin of lamb, and cut it into cutlets about ¾ inch in thickness. Have ready a bright clear fire; lay the cutlets on a gridiron, and broil them of a nice pale brown, turning them when required. Season them with pepper and salt; serve very hot and quickly, and garnish with crisped parsley, or place them on mashed potatoes. Asparagus, spinach, or peas are the favourite accompaniments to lamb chops. *Time.*—About 8 or 10 minutes. *Average cost,* 1s. per lb. *Sufficient.*—Allow 2 cutlets to each person. *Seasonable* from Easter to Michaelmas.

LAMB,CutletsandSpinach(anEntrée).

Ingredients.—8 cutlets, egg and bread-crumbs, salt and pepper to taste, a little clarified butter. *Mode.*—Cut the cutlets from a neck of lamb, and shape them by cutting off the thick part of the chine-bone. Trim off most of the fat and all the skin, and scrape the top part of the bones quite clean. Brush the cutlets over with egg, sprinkle them with bread-crumbs, and season with pepper and salt. Now dip them into clarified butter, sprinkle over a few more bread-crumbs, and fry them over a sharp fire, turning them when required. Lay them before the fire to drain, and arrange them on a dish with spinach in the centre, which should be previously well boiled, drained, chopped, and seasoned. *Time.*—About 7 or 8 minutes. *Average cost*, 10*d*. per lb. *Sufficient* for 4 persons. *Seasonable* from Easter to Michaelmas.

Note.—Peas, asparagus, or French beans, may be substituted for the spinach; or lamb cutlets may be served with stewed cucumbers, Soubise sauce, &c., &c.

LAMB, Roast Fore-quarter of.

FORE-QUARTER OF LAMB.

Ingredients.—Lamb, a little salt. *Mode.*—To obtain the flavour of lamb in perfection, it should not be long kept; time to cool is all that it requires; and though the meat may be somewhat thready, the juices and flavour will be infinitely superior to that of lamb that has been killed 2 or 3 days. Make up the fire in good time, that it may be clear and brisk when the joint is put down. Place it at a sufficient distance to prevent the fat from burning, and baste it constantly till the moment of serving. Lamb should be very *thoroughly* done without being dried up, and not the slightest appearance of red gravy should be visible, as in roast mutton: this rule is applicable to all young white meats. Serve with a little gravy made in the dripping-pan, the same as for other roasts, and send to table with it a tureen of mint sauce, and a fresh salad. A cut lemon, a small piece of fresh butter, and a little cayenne, should also be placed on the table, so that when the carver separates the shoulder from the ribs, they may be ready for his use; if, however, he should not be very expert, we would recommend that the cook should divide these joints nicely before coming to table. *Time.*—Fore-quarter of lamb weighing 10 lbs., 1¾ to 2 hours. *Average cost*, 10*d*. to 1*s*. per lb. *Sufficient* for 7 or 8 persons. *Seasonable.*—Grass lamb, from Easter to Michaelmas.

LAMB'S FRY.

Ingredients.—1 lb. of lamb's fry, 3 pints of water, egg and bread-crumbs, 1 teaspoonful of chopped parsley, salt and pepper to taste. *Mode.*—Boil the fry for ¼ hour in the above proportion of water, take it out and dry it in a cloth; grate some bread down finely, mix with it a teaspoonful of chopped parsley and a high seasoning of pepper and salt. Brush the fry lightly over with the yolk of an egg, sprinkle over the bread-crumbs, and fry for 5 minutes. Serve very hot on a napkin in a dish, and garnish with plenty of crisped parsley. *Time.*—¼ hour to simmer the fry, 5 minutes to fry it. *Average cost*, 10d. per lb. *Sufficient* for 2 or 3 persons. *Seasonable* from Easter to Michaelmas.

LAMB, Hashed, and Broiled Blade-Bone.

[COLD MEAT COOKERY.] *Ingredients.*—The remains of a cold shoulder of lamb, pepper and salt to taste, 2 oz. of butter, about ½ pint of stock or gravy, 1 tablespoonful of shalot vinegar, 3 or 4 pickled gherkins. *Mode.*—Take the blade-bone from the shoulder, and cut the meat into collops as neatly as possible. Season the bone with pepper and salt, pour a little oiled butter over it, and place it in the oven to warm through. Put the stock into a stewpan, add the ketchup and shalot vinegar, and lay in the pieces of lamb. Let these heat gradually through, but do not allow them to boil. Take the blade-bone out of the oven, and place it on a gridiron over a sharp fire to brown. Slice the gherkins, put them into the hash, and dish it with the blade-bone in the centre. It may be garnished with croûtons or sippets of toasted bread. *Time.*—Altogether ½ hour. *Average cost*, exclusive of the meat, 4d. *Seasonable.*—Houselamb, from Christmas to March; grass lamb, from Easter to Michaelmas.

LAMB, Boiled Leg of, à la Béchamel.

Ingredients.—Leg of lamb, Béchamel sauce. *Mode.*—Do not choose a very large joint, but one weighing about 5 lbs. Have ready a saucepan of boiling water, into which plunge the lamb, and when it boils up again, draw it to the side of the fire, and let the water cool a little. Then stew very gently for about 1¼ hour, reckoning from the time that the water begins to simmer. Make some Béchamel, dish the lamb, pour the sauce over it, and garnish with tufts of boiled cauliflower or carrots. When liked, melted butter may be substituted for the Béchamel: this is a more simple method, but not nearly so nice. Send to table with it some of the sauce in a tureen, and boiled cauliflowers or spinach, with whichever vegetable the dish is garnished. *Time.*—1¼ hour after the water simmers. *Average cost*, 10*d.* to 1*s.* per lb. *Sufficient* for 4 or 5 persons. *Seasonable* from Easter to Michaelmas.

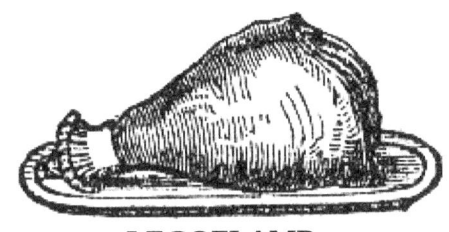

LEGOFLAMB.

LAMB, Roast Leg of.

Ingredients.—Lamb, a little salt. *Mode.*—Place the joint at a good distance from the fire at first, and baste well the whole time it is cooking. When nearly done, draw it nearer the fire to acquire a nice brown colour. Sprinkle a little fine salt over the meat, empty the dripping-pan of its contents; pour in a little boiling water, and strain this over the meat. Serve with mint sauce and a fresh salad, and for vegetables send peas, spinach, or cauliflowers to table with it. *Time.*—A leg of lamb weighing 5 lbs., 1½ hour. *Average cost*, 10*d.* to 1*s.* a pound. *Sufficient* for 4 or 5 persons. *Seasonable* from Easter to Michaelmas.

LOINOFLAMB.

LAMB, Braised Loin of.

Ingredients.—1 loin of lamb, a few slices of bacon, 1 bunch of green onions, 5 or 6 young carrots, a bunch of savoury herbs, 2 blades of pounded mace, 1 pint of stock, salt to taste. *Mode.*—Bone a loin of lamb, and line the bottom of a stewpan just capable of holding it, with a few thin slices of fat bacon; add the remaining ingredients, cover the meat with a few more slices of bacon, pour in the stock, and simmer very *gently* for 2 hours; take it up, dry it, strain and reduce the gravy to a glaze, with which glaze the meat, and serve it either on stewed peas, spinach, or stewed cucumbers. *Time.*—2 hours. *Average cost*, 11*d*. per lb. *Sufficient* for 4 or 5 persons. *Seasonable* from Easter to Michaelmas.

SADDLE OF LAMB.

LAMB, Roast Saddle of.

Ingredients.—Lamb; a little salt. *Mode.*—This joint is now very much in vogue, and is generally considered a nice one for a small party. Have ready a clear brisk fire; put down the joint at a little distance, to prevent the fat from scorching, and keep it well basted all the time it is cooking. Serve with mint sauce and a fresh salad, and send to table with it either peas, cauliflowers, or spinach. *Time.*—A small saddle, 1½ hour; a large one, 2 hours. *Average cost*, 10*d*. to 1*s*. per lb. *Sufficient* for 5 or 6 persons. *Seasonable* from Easter to Michaelmas.

RIBS OF LAMB.

Note.—Loin and ribs of lamb are roasted in the same manner, and served with the same sauces as the above. A loin will take about 1¼ hour; ribs, from 1 to 1¼ hour.

LAMB, Roast Shoulder of.

Ingredients.—Lamb; a little salt. *Mode.*—Have ready a clear brisk fire, and put down the joint at a sufficient distance from it, that the fat may not burn. Keep constantly basting until done, and serve with a little gravy made in the dripping-pan, and send mint sauce to table with it. Peas, spinach, or cauliflowers are the usual vegetables served with lamb, and also a fresh salad. *Time.*—A shoulder of lamb rather more than 1 hour. *Average cost*, 10*d.* to 1*s.* per lb. *Sufficient* for 4 or 5 persons. *Seasonable* from Easter to Michaelmas.

LAMB, Shoulder of, Stuffed.

Ingredients.—Shoulder of lamb, forcemeat, trimmings of veal or beef, 2 onions, ½ head of celery, 1 faggot of savoury herbs, a few slices of fat bacon, 1 quart of stock. *Mode.*—Take the blade-bone out of a shoulder of lamb, fill up its place with forcemeat, and sew it up with coarse thread. Put it into a stewpan with a few slices of bacon under and over the lamb, and add the remaining ingredients. Stew very gently for rather more than 2 hours. Reduce the gravy, with which glaze the meat, and serve with peas, stewed cucumbers, or sorrel sauce. *Time.*—Rather more than 2 hours. *Average cost*, 10*d.* to 1*s.* per lb. *Sufficient* for 4 or 5 persons. *Seasonable* from Easter to Michaelmas.

LANDRAIL, Roast, or Corn-Crake.

LANDRAILS.

Ingredients.—3 or 4 birds, butter, fried bread-crumbs. *Mode.*—Pluck and draw the birds, wipe them inside and out with damp cloths, and truss them in the following manner: Bring the head round under the wing, and the thighs close to the sides; pass a skewer through them and the body, and keep the legs straight. Roast them before a clear fire, keep them well basted, and serve on fried bread-crumbs, with a tureen of brown gravy. When liked, bread-sauce may also be sent to table with them. *Time.*—12 to 20 minutes. *Average cost.*—Seldom bought. *Sufficient.*—Allow 4 for a dish. *Seasonable* from August 12th to the middle of September.

LANDRAIL, to Carve.

Landrail, being trussed like Snipe, with the exception of its being drawn, may be carved in the same manner.

LARD, to Melt.

Melt the inner fat of the pig, by putting it in a stone jar, and placing this in a saucepan of boiling water, previously stripping off the skin. Let it simmer gently over a bright fire, and, as it melts, pour it carefully from the sediment. Put it into small jars or bladders for use, and keep it in a cool place. The flead or inside fat of the pig, before it is melted, makes exceedingly light crust, and is particularly wholesome. It may be preserved a length of time by salting it well, and occasionally changing the brine. When wanted for use, wash and wipe it, and it will answer for making into paste as well as fresh lard. *Average cost*, 10*d.* per lb.

LARDING.

Ingredients.—Bacon and larding-needle. *Mode.*—Bacon for larding should be firm and fat, and ought to be cured without any saltpetre, as this reddens white meats. Lay it on a table, the rinds downwards; trim off any rusty part, and cut it into slices of an equal thickness. Place the slices one on the top of another, and cut them evenly into narrow strips, so arranging it that every piece of bacon is of the same size. Bacon for fricandeaux, poultry, and game, should be about 2 inches in length, and rather more than one-eighth of an inch in width. If for larding fillets of beef or loin of veal, the pieces of bacon must be thicker. The following recipe of Soyer is, we think, very explicit; and any cook, by following the directions here given, may be able to lard, if not well, sufficiently for general use:—

BACON FOR LARDING, AND LARDING-NEEDLE.

"Have the fricandeau trimmed; lay it, lengthwise, upon a clean napkin across your hand, forming a kind of bridge with your thumb at the part where you are about to commence; then with the point of the larding-needle make three distinct lines across, ½ inch apart; run the needle into the third line, at the farther side of the fricandeau, and bring it out at the first, placing one of the lardoons in it; draw the needle through, leaving out ¼ inch of the bacon at each line; proceed thus to the end of the row; then make another line, ½ inch distant, stick in another row of lardoons, bringing them out at the second line, leaving the ends of the bacon out all the same length; make the next row again at the same distance, bringing the ends out between the lardoons of the first row, proceeding in this manner until the whole surface is larded in chequered rows. Everything else is larded in a similar way; and, in the case of poultry, hold the breast over a charcoal fire for one minute, or dip it into boiling water, in order to make the flesh firm."

LARK PIE (an Entrée).

Ingredients.—A few thin slices of beef, the same of bacon, 9 larks, flour; for stuffing, 1 teacupful of bread-crumbs, ½ teaspoonful of minced lemon-peel, 1 teaspoonful of minced parsley, 1 egg, salt and pepper to taste, 1 teaspoonful of chopped shalot, ½ pint of weak stock or water, puff-paste. *Mode.*—Make a stuffing of bread-crumbs, minced lemon-peel, parsley, and the yolk of an egg, all of which should be well mixed together; roll the larks in flour, and stuff them. Line the bottom of a pie-dish with a few slices of beef and bacon; over these place the larks, and season with salt, pepper, minced parsley, and chopped shalot, in the above proportion. Pour in the stock or water, cover with crust, and bake for an hour in a moderate oven. During the time the pie is baking, shake it 2 or 3 times, to assist in thickening the gravy, and serve very hot. Time.—1 hour. *Average cost*, 1s. 6d. per dozen. *Sufficient* for 5 or 6 persons. *Seasonable.*—In full season in November.

LARKS, Roast.

Ingredients.—Larks, egg and bread-crumbs, fresh butter. *Mode.*—These birds are by many persons esteemed a great delicacy, and may be either roasted or broiled. Pick, gut, and clean them; when they are trussed, brush them over with the yolk of an egg; sprinkle with bread-crumbs, and roast them before a quick fire; baste them continually with fresh butter, and keep sprinkling with the bread-crumbs until the birds are well covered. Dish them on bread-crumbs fried in clarified butter, and garnish the dish with slices of lemon. Broiled larks are also very excellent: they should be cooked over a clear fire, and would take about 10 minutes or ¼ hour. *Time.*—¼ hour to roast; 10 minutes to broil. *Seasonable.*—In full season in November.

Note.—Larks may also be plainly roasted, without covering them with egg and bread-crumbs; they should be dished on fried crumbs.

LEEKSOUP.

Ingredients.—A sheep's head, 3 quarts of water, 12 leeks cut small, pepper and salt to taste, oatmeal to thicken. *Mode.*—Prepare the head, either by skinning or cleaning the skin very nicely; split it in two; take out the brains, and put it into boiling water; add the leeks and seasoning, and simmer very gently for 4 hours. Mix smoothly, with cold water, as much oatmeal as will make the soup tolerably thick; pour it into the soup; continue stirring till the whole is blended and well done, and serve. *Time.*—4½ hours. *Average cost*, 4*d*. per quart. *Seasonable* in winter. *Sufficient* for 10 persons.

LEMONBISCUITS.

Ingredients.—1¼ lb. of flour, ¾ lb. of loaf sugar, 6 oz. of fresh butter, 4 eggs, 1 oz. of lemon-peel, 2 dessertspoonfuls of lemon-juice. *Mode.*—Rub the flour into the butter; stir in the pounded sugar and very finely-minced lemon-peel, and when these ingredients are thoroughly mixed, add the eggs, which should be previously well whisked, and the lemon-juice. Beat the mixture well for a minute or two, then drop it from a spoon on to a buttered tin, about 2 inches apart, as the cakes will spread when they get warm; place the tin in the oven, and bake the cakes of a pale brown from 15 to 20 minutes. *Time.*—15 to 20 minutes. *Average cost*, 1*s*. 6*d*. *Seasonable* at any time.

LEMONBLANCMANGE.

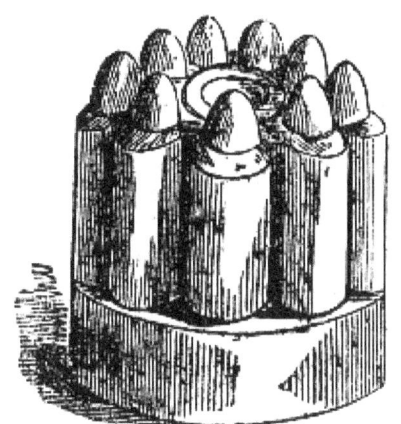
BLANCMANGEMOULD.

Ingredients.—1 quart of milk, the yolks of 4 eggs, 3 oz. of ground rice, 6 oz. of pounded sugar, 1½ oz. of fresh butter, the rind of 1 lemon, the juice of 2, ½ oz. of gelatine. *Mode.*—Make a custard with the yolks of the eggs and ½ pint of the milk, and when done, put it into a basin; put half the remainder of the milk into a saucepan with the ground rice, fresh butter, lemon-rind, and 3 oz. of the sugar, and let these ingredients boil until the mixture is stiff, stirring them continually; when done, pour it into the bowl where the custard is, mixing both well together. Put the gelatine with the rest of the milk into a saucepan, and let it stand by the side of the fire to dissolve; boil for a minute or two, stir carefully into the basin, adding 3 oz. more of pounded sugar. When cold, stir in the lemon-juice, which should be carefully strained, and pour the mixture into a well-oiled mould, leaving out the lemon-peel, and set the mould in a pan of cold water until wanted for table. Use eggs that have rich-looking yolks; and, should the weather be very warm, rather a larger proportion of gelatine must be allowed. *Time.*—Altogether, ½ hour. *Average cost*, 1*s.* 6*d. Sufficient* to fill 2 small moulds. *Seasonable* at any time.

LEMONCAKE.

CAKE-MOULD.

Ingredients.—10 eggs, 3 tablespoonfuls of orange-flower water, ¾ lb. of pounded loaf sugar, 1 lemon, ¾ lb. of flour. *Mode.*—Separate the whites from the yolks of the eggs; whisk the former to a stiff froth; add the orange-flower water, the sugar, grated lemon-rind, and mix these ingredients well together. Then beat the yolks of the eggs, and add them, with the lemon-juice, to the whites, &c.; dredge in the flour gradually; keep beating the mixture well; put it into a buttered mould, and bake the cake about an hour, or rather longer. The addition of a little butter, beaten to a cream, we think, would improve this cake. *Time.*—About 1 hour. *Average cost,* 1*s.* 4*d.* *Seasonable* at any time.

LEMONCHEESECAKES.

Ingredients.—¼ lb. of butter, 1 lb. of loaf sugar, 6 eggs, the rind of 2 lemons and the juice of 3. *Mode.*—Put all the ingredients into a stewpan, carefully grating the lemon-rind and straining the juice. Keep stirring the mixture over the fire until the sugar is dissolved, and it begins to thicken: when of the consistency of honey, it is done; then put it into small jars, and keep in a dry place. This mixture will remain good 3 or 4 months. When made into cheesecakes, add a few pounded almonds, or candied peel, or grated sweet biscuit; line some patty-pans with good puff-paste, rather more than half fill them with the mixture, and bake for about ¼ hour in a good brisk oven. *Time.*—¼ hour. *Average cost,* 1*s.* 4*d.* *Sufficient* for 24 cheesecakes. *Seasonable* at any time.

LEMONCREAM.

Ingredients.—1 pint of cream, the yolks of two eggs, ¼ lb. of white sugar, 1 large lemon, 1 oz. of isinglass. *Mode.*—Put the cream into a *lined* saucepan with the sugar, lemon-peel, and isinglass, and simmer these over a gentle fire for about 10 minutes, stirring them all the time. Strain the cream into a jug, add the yolks of eggs, which should be well beaten, and put the jug into a saucepan of boiling water; stir the mixture one way until it thickens, *but do not allow it to boil*; take it off the fire, and keep stirring it until nearly cold. Strain the lemon-juice into a basin, gradually pour on it the cream, and *stir it well* until the juice is well mixed with it. Have ready a well-oiled mould, pour the cream into it, and let it remain until perfectly set.

When required for table, loosen the edges with a small blunt knife, put a dish on the top of the mould, turn it over quickly, and the cream should easily slip away. *Time.*—10 minutes to boil the cream; about 10 minutes to stir it over the fire in the jug. *Average cost,* with cream at 1*s.* per pint, and the best isinglass, 3*s.* 6*d. Sufficient* to fill 1½ pint mould. *Seasonable* at any time.

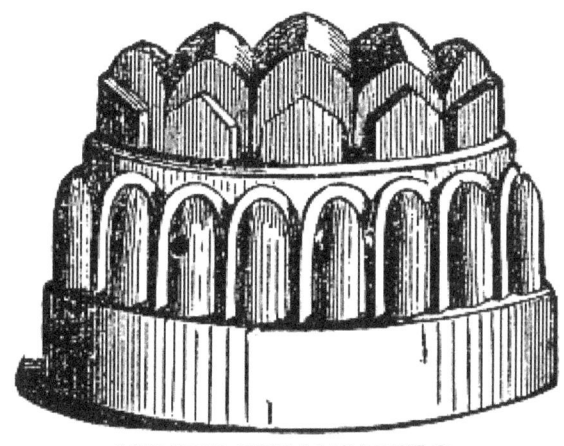

LEMON-CREAM MOULD.

LEMON CREAM, Economical.

Ingredients.—1 quart of milk, 8 bitter almonds, 2 oz. of gelatine, 2 large lemons, ¾ lb. of lump sugar, the yolks of 6 eggs. *Mode.*—Put the milk into a lined saucepan with the almonds, which should be well pounded in a mortar, the gelatine, lemon-rind, and lump sugar, and boil these ingredients for about 5 minutes. Beat up the yolks of the eggs, strain the milk into a jug, add the eggs, and pour the mixture backwards and forwards a few times, until nearly cold; then stir briskly to it the lemon-juice, which should be strained, and keep stirring until the cream is almost cold; put it into an oiled mould, and let it remain until perfectly set. The lemon-juice must not be added to the cream when it is warm, and should be well stirred after it is put in. *Time.*—5 minutes to boil the milk. *Average cost*, 2*s.* 5*d. Sufficient* to fill two 1½ pint moulds. *Seasonable* at any time.

LEMON CREAMS, Very Good.

Ingredients.—1 pint of cream, 2 dozen sweet almonds, 3 glasses of sherry, the rind and juice of 2 lemons, sugar to taste. *Mode.*—Blanch and chop the almonds, and put them into a jug with the cream; in another jug put the sherry, lemon-rind, strained juice, and sufficient pounded sugar to sweeten the whole nicely. Pour rapidly from one jug to the other till the mixture is well frothed; then pour it into jelly-glasses, omitting the lemon-rind. This is a very cool and delicious sweet for summer, and may be made less rich by omitting the almonds and substituting orange or raisin wine for the sherry. *Time.*—Altogether, ½ hour. *Average cost*, with cream at 1*s.* per pint, 3*s. Sufficient* to fill 12 glasses. *Seasonable* at any time.

LEMONCREAMS, or Custards.

Ingredients.—5 oz. of loaf sugar, 2 pints of boiling water, the rind of 1 lemon and the juice of 3, the yolks of 8 eggs. *Mode.*—Make a quart of lemonade in the following manner:—Dissolve the sugar in the boiling water, having previously, with part of the sugar, rubbed off the lemon-rind, and add the strained juice. Strain the lemonade into a saucepan, and add the yolks of the eggs, which should be well beaten; stir this *one way* over the fire until the mixture thickens, but do not allow it to boil, and serve in custard glasses, or on a glass dish. After the boiling water is poured on the sugar and lemon, it should stand covered for about ½ hour before the eggs are added to it, that the flavour of the rind may be extracted. *Time.*—½ hour to make the lemonade; about 10 minutes to stir the custard over the fire. *Average cost*, 1*s. Sufficient* to fill 12 to 14 custard glasses. *Seasonable* at any time.

LEMONDUMPLINGS.

Ingredients.—½ lb. of grated bread, ¼ lb. of chopped suet, ¼ lb. of moist sugar, 2 eggs, 1 large lemon. *Mode.*—Mix the bread, suet, and moist sugar well together, adding the lemon-peel, which should be very finely minced. Moisten with the eggs and strained lemon-juice; stir well, and put the mixture into small buttered cups. Tie them down and boil for ¾ hour. Turn them out on a dish, strew sifted sugar over them, and serve with wine sauce. *Time.*—¾ hour. *Average cost*, 7*d. Sufficient* for 6 dumplings. *Seasonable* at any time.

LEMON DUMPLINGS.

LEMON JELLY.

Ingredients.—6 lemons, ¾ lb. of lump sugar, 1 pint of water, 1¼ oz. of isinglass, ¼ pint of sherry. *Mode.*—Peel 3 of the lemons, pour ½ pint of boiling water on the rind, and let it infuse for ½ hour; put the sugar, isinglass, and ½ pint of water into a lined saucepan, and boil these ingredients for 20 minutes; then put in the strained lemon-juice, the strained infusion of the rind, and bring the whole to the point of boiling; skim well, add the wine, and run the jelly through a bag; pour it into a mould that has been wetted or soaked in water; put it in ice, if convenient, where let it remain until required for table. Previously to adding the lemon-juice to the other ingredients, ascertain that it is very nicely strained, as, if this is not properly attended to, it is liable to make the jelly thick and muddy. As this jelly is very pale, and almost colourless, it answers very well for moulding with a jelly of any bright hue; for instance, half a jelly bright red, and the other half made of the above, would have a very good effect. Lemon jelly may also be made with calf's-feet stock, allowing the juice of 3 lemons to every pint of stock. *Time.*—Altogether, 1 hour. *Average cost*, with the best isinglass, 3*s.* 6*d. Sufficient* to fill 1½ pint mould. *Seasonable* at any time.

LEMON MINCEMEAT.

Ingredients.—2 large lemons, 6 large apples, ½ lb. of suet, 1 lb. of currants, ½ lb. of sugar, 2 oz. of candied lemon-peel, 1 oz. of citron, mixed spice to taste. *Mode.*—Pare the lemons, squeeze them, and boil the peel until tender enough to mash. Add to the mashed lemon-peel the apples, which should be pared, cored, and minced; the chopped suet, currants, sugar, sliced peel, and spice. Strain the lemon-juice to these ingredients, stir the mixture well, and put it in a jar with a closely-fitting lid. Stir occasionally, and in a week or 10 days the mincemeat will be ready for use.

Average cost, 2s. *Sufficient* for 18 large or 24 small pies. *Seasonable.*—Make this about the beginning of December.

LEMON-PEEL.

This contains an essential oil of a very high flavour and fragrance, and is consequently esteemed both a wholesome and agreeable stomachic. It is used, as will be seen by many recipes in this book, as an ingredient for flavouring a number of various dishes. Under the name of candied lemon-peel, it is cleared of the pulp and preserved in sugar, when it becomes an excellent sweetmeat.

LEMON PUDDING, Baked.

Ingredients.—The yolks of 4 eggs, 4 oz. of pounded sugar, 1 lemon, ¼ lb. of butter, puff-crust. *Mode.*—Beat the eggs to a froth; mix with them the sugar and warmed butter; stir these ingredients well together, putting in the grated rind and strained juice of the lemon-peel. Line a shallow dish with puff-paste; put in the mixture, and bake in a moderate oven for 40 minutes; turn the pudding out of the dish, strew over it sifted sugar, and serve. *Time.*—40 minutes. *Average cost*, 10d. *Sufficient* for 5 or 6 persons. *Seasonable* at any time.

LEMON PUDDING, Baked.

Ingredients.—10 oz. of bread-crumbs, 2 pints of milk, 2 oz. of butter, 1 lemon, ¼ lb. of pounded sugar, 4 eggs, 1 tablespoonful of brandy. *Mode.*—Bring the milk to the boiling point, stir in the butter, and pour these hot over the bread-crumbs; add the sugar and very finely-minced lemon-peel; beat the eggs, and stir these in with the brandy to the other ingredients; put a paste round the dish, and bake for ¾ hour. *Time.*—¾ hour. *Average cost*, 1s. 2d. *Sufficient* for 6 or 7 persons. *Seasonable* at any time.

LEMON PUDDING, Baked (Very Rich).

Ingredients.—The rind and juice of 2 large lemons, ½ lb. of loaf sugar, ¼ pint of cream, the yolks of 8 eggs, 2 oz. of almonds, ½ lb. of butter, melted. *Mode.*—Mix the pounded sugar with the cream and add the yolks of eggs and the butter, which should be previously warmed. Blanch and pound the almonds, and put these, with the grated rind and strained juice of the lemons, to the other ingredients. Stir all well together; line a dish with puff-paste, put in the mixture, and bake for 1 hour. *Time.*—1 hour. *Average cost*, 2*s*. *Sufficient* for 6 or 7 persons. *Seasonable* at any time.

LEMON PUDDING, Boiled.

Ingredients.—½ lb. of chopped suet, ¾ lb. of bread-crumbs, 2 small lemons, 6 oz. of moist sugar, ¼ lb. of flour, 2 eggs, milk. *Mode.*—Mix the suet, bread-crumbs, sugar, and flour well together, adding the lemon-peel, which should be very finely minced, and the juice, which should be strained. When these ingredients are well mixed, moisten with the eggs and sufficient milk to make the pudding of the consistency of thick batter; put it into a well-buttered mould, and boil for 3½ hours; turn it out, strew sifted sugar over, and serve with wine sauce, or not, at pleasure. *Time.*—3½ hours. *Average cost*, 1*s*. *Sufficient* for 7 or 8 persons. *Seasonable* at any time.

Note.—This pudding may also be baked, and will be found very good. It will take about 2 hours.

LEMON PUDDING, Plain.

Ingredients.—¾ lb. of flour, 6 oz. of lard or dripping, the juice of 1 large lemon, 1 teaspoonful of flour, sugar. *Mode.*—Make the above proportions of flour and lard into a smooth paste, and roll it out to the thickness of about ½ an inch. Squeeze the lemon-juice, strain it into a cup, stir the flour into it, and as much moist sugar as will make it into a stiff and thick paste; spread this mixture over the paste, roll it up, secure the ends, and tie the pudding in a floured cloth. Boil for 2 hours. *Time.*—2 hours. *Average cost*, 7*d*. *Sufficient* for 5 or 6 persons. *Seasonable* at any time.

LEMON SAUCE, for Boiled Fowl.

Ingredients.—1 small lemon, ¾ pint of melted butter. *Mode.*—Cut the lemon into very thin slices, and these again into very small dice. Have ready ¾ pint of melted butter, put in the lemon; let it just simmer, but not boil, and pour it over the fowls. *Time.*—1 minute to simmer. *Average cost*, 6d. *Sufficient* for a pair of large fowls.

LEMON WHITE SAUCE, for Fowls, Fricassees, &c.

Ingredients.—¾ pint of cream, the rind and juice of 1 lemon, ½ teaspoonful of whole white pepper, 1 sprig of lemon thyme, 3 oz. of butter, 1 dessertspoonful of flour, 1 teacupful of white stock; salt to taste. *Mode.*—Put the cream into a very clean saucepan (a lined one is best), with the lemon-peel, pepper, and thyme, and let these infuse for ½ hour, when simmer gently for a few minutes, or until there is a nice flavour of lemon. Strain it, and add a thickening of butter and flour in the above proportions; stir this well in, and put in the lemon-juice at the moment of serving; mix the stock with the cream, and add a little salt. This sauce should not boil after the cream and stock are mixed together. *Time.*—Altogether, ¾ hour. *Average cost*, 1s. 6d. *Sufficient*, this quantity, for a pair of large boiled fowls.

Note.—Where the expense of the cream is objected to, milk may be substituted for it. In this case, an additional dessertspoonful, or rather more, of flour must be added.

LEMON SAUCE, for Sweet Puddings.

Ingredients.—The rind and juice of 1 lemon, 1 tablespoonful of flour, 1 oz. of butter, 1 large wineglassful of sherry, 1 wineglassful of water, sugar to taste, the yolks of 4 eggs. *Mode.*—Rub the rind of the lemon on to some lumps of sugar; squeeze out the juice, and strain it; put the butter and flour into a saucepan, stir them over the fire, and when of a pale brown, add the wine, water, and strained lemon-juice. Crush the lumps of sugar that were rubbed on the lemon; stir these into the sauce, which should be very sweet. When these ingredients are well mixed, and the sugar is melted, put in the beaten yolks of 4 eggs; keep stirring the sauce until it thickens, when serve. Do not, on any account, allow it to boil, or it will curdle, and be entirely spoiled. *Time.*—Altogether, 15 minutes. *Average cost*, 1s. 2d. *Sufficient* for 7 or 8 persons.

LEMON SPONGE.

Ingredients.—2 oz. of isinglass, 1¾ pint of water, ¾ lb. of pounded sugar, the juice of 5 lemons, the rind of 1, the whites of 3 eggs. *Mode.*—Dissolve the isinglass in the water, strain it into a saucepan, and add the sugar, lemon-rind, and juice. Boil the whole from 10 to 15 minutes; strain it again, and let it stand till it is cold and begins to stiffen. Beat the whites of the eggs, put them to it, and whisk the mixture till it is quite white; put it into a mould which has been previously wetted, and let it remain until perfectly set; then turn it out, and garnish it according to taste. *Time.*—10 to 15 minutes. *Average cost*, with the best isinglass, 4*s*. *Sufficient* to fill a quart mould. *Seasonable* at any time.

LEMON SYRUP.

Ingredients.—2 lbs. of loaf sugar, 2 pints of water, 1 oz. of citric acid, ½ drachm of essence of lemon. *Mode.*—Boil the sugar and water together for ¼ hour, and put it into a basin, where let it remain till cold. Beat the citric acid to a powder, mix the essence of lemon with it, then add these two ingredients to the syrup; mix well, and bottle for use. Two tablespoonfuls of the syrup are sufficient for a tumbler of cold water, and will be found a very refreshing summer drink. *Sufficient.*—2 tablespoonfuls of syrup to a tumblerful of cold water.

LEMONS, to Pickle, with the Peel on.

Ingredients.—6 lemons, 2 quarts of boiling water; to each quart of vinegar allow ½ oz. of cloves, ½ oz. of white pepper, 1 oz. of bruised ginger, ¼ oz. of mace and chilies, 1 oz. of mustard-seed, ½ stick of sliced horseradish, a few cloves of garlic. *Mode.*—Put the lemons into a brine that will bear an egg; let them remain in it 6 days, stirring them every day; have ready 2 quarts of boiling water, put in the lemons, and allow them to boil for ¼ hour; take them out, and let them lie in a cloth until perfectly dry and cold. Boil up sufficient vinegar to cover the lemons, with all the above ingredients, allowing the same proportion as stated to each quart of vinegar. Pack the lemons in a jar, pour over the vinegar, &c. boiling hot, and tie down with a bladder. They will be fit for use in about 12 months, or rather sooner. *Seasonable.*—This should be made from November to April.

LEMONS, to Pickle, without the Peel.

Ingredients.—6 lemons, 1 lb. of fine salt; to each quart of vinegar, the same ingredients as in the last recipe. *Mode.*—Peel the lemons, slit each one down 3 times, so as not to divide them, and rub the salt well into the divisions; place them in a pan, where they must remain for a week, turning them every other day; then put them in a Dutch oven before a clear fire until the salt has become perfectly dry; then arrange them in a jar. Pour over sufficient boiling vinegar to cover them, to which have been added the ingredients mentioned in the foregoing recipe; tie down closely, and in about 9 months they will be fit for use. *Seasonable.*—The best time to make this is from November to April.

Note.—After this pickle has been made from 4 to 5 months, the liquor may be strained and bottled, and will be found an excellent lemon ketchup.

LEMON WINE.

Ingredients.—To 4½ gallons of water allow the pulp of 50 lemons, the rind of 25, 16 lbs. of loaf sugar, ½ oz. of isinglass, 1 bottle of brandy. *Mode.*—Peel and slice the lemons, but use only the rind of 25 of them, and put them into the cold water. Let it stand 8 or 9 days, squeezing the lemons well every day; then strain the water off and put it into a cask with the sugar. Let it work some time, and when it has ceased working, put in the isinglass. Stop the cask down; in about six months put in the brandy and bottle the wine off. *Seasonable.*—The best time to make this is in January or February, when lemons are best and cheapest.

LEMONADE.

Ingredients.—The rind of two lemons, the juice of 3 large or 4 small ones, ½ lb. of loaf sugar, 1 quart of boiling water. *Mode.*—Rub some of the sugar, in lumps, on 2 of the lemons until they have imbibed all the oil from them, and put it with the remainder of the sugar into a jug; add the lemon-juice (but no pips), and pour over the whole a quart of boiling water. When the sugar is dissolved, strain the lemonade through a fine sieve or piece of muslin, and, when cool, it will be ready for use. The lemonade will be much improved by having the white of an egg beaten up in it; a little sherry mixed with it, also, makes this beverage much nicer. *Average cost*, 6*d.* per quart.

LEMONADE, Nourishing.

Ingredients.—1½ pint of boiling water, the juice of 4 lemons, the rinds of 2, ½ pint of sherry, 4 eggs, 6 oz. of loaf sugar. *Mode.*—Pare off the lemon-rind thinly, put it into a jug with the sugar, and pour over the boiling water. Let it cool, then strain it; add the wine, lemon-juice, and eggs, previously well beaten, and also strained, and the beverage will be ready for use. If thought desirable, the quantity of sherry and water could be lessened, and milk substituted for them. To obtain the flavour of the lemon-rind properly, a few lumps of the sugar should be rubbed over it, until some of the yellow is absorbed. *Time.*—Altogether 1 hour to make it. *Average cost*, 1*s.* 8*d. Sufficient* to make 2½ pints of lemonade. *Seasonable*, at any time.

LETTUCES.

These form one of the principal ingredients to summer salads; they should be blanched, and be eaten young. They are seldom served in any other way, but may be stewed and sent to table in a good brown gravy flavoured with lemon-juice. In preparing them for a salad, carefully wash them free from dirt, pick off all the decayed and outer leaves, and dry them thoroughly by shaking them in a cloth. Cut off the stalks, and either halve or cut the lettuces into small pieces. The manner of cutting them up entirely depends on the salad for which they are intended. In France, the lettuces are sometimes merely wiped with a cloth and not washed, the cooks there declaring that the act of washing them injuriously affects the pleasant crispness of the plant: in this case scrupulous attention must be paid to each leaf, and the grit thoroughly wiped away. *Average cost*, when cheapest, 1*d.* each. *Sufficient.*—Allow 2 lettuces for 4 or 5 persons. *Seasonable* from March to the end of August, but may be had all the year.

LEVERET, to Dress a.

Ingredients.—2 leverets, butter, flour. *Mode.*—Leverets should be trussed in the same manner as a hare, but they do not require stuffing. Roast them before a clear fire, and keep them well basted all the time they are cooking. A few minutes before serving, dredge them lightly with flour, and froth them nicely. Serve with plain gravy in the dish, and send to table red-currant jelly with them. *Time.*—½ to ¾ hour. *Average cost*, in full season, 4s. each. *Sufficient* for 5 or 6 persons. *Seasonable* from May to August, but cheapest in July and August.

LIAISON OF EGGS, for Thickening Sauces.

Ingredients.—The yolks of 3 eggs, 8 tablespoonfuls of milk or cream. *Mode.*—Beat up the yolks of the eggs, to which add the milk, and strain the whole through a hair-sieve. When the liaison is being added to the sauce it is intended to thicken, care must be exercised to keep stirring it during the whole time, or, otherwise, the eggs will curdle. It should only just simmer, but not boil.

LIQUEUR JELLY.

Ingredients.—1 lb. of lump sugar, 2 oz. of isinglass, 1½ pint of water, the juice of 2 lemons, ¼ pint of liqueur. *Mode.*—Put the sugar, with 1 pint of the water, into a stewpan, and boil them gently by the side of the fire until there is no scum remaining, which must be carefully removed as fast as it rises. Boil the isinglass with the other ½ pint of water, and skim it carefully in the same manner. Strain the lemon-juice, and add it, with the clarified isinglass, to the syrup; put in the liqueur, and bring the whole to the boiling-point. Let the saucepan remain covered by the side of the fire for a few minutes; then pour the jelly through a bag, put it into a mould, and set the mould in ice until required for table. Dip the mould in hot water, wipe the outside, loosen the jelly by passing a knife round the edges, and turn it out carefully on a dish. Noyeau, Maraschino, Curaçoa, brandy, or any kind of liqueur, answers for this jelly; and, when made with isinglass, liqueur jellies are usually prepared as directed above. *Time.*—10 minutes to boil the sugar and water. *Average cost*, with the best isinglass, 3s. 6d. *Sufficient* to fill a quart mould. *Seasonable* at any time.

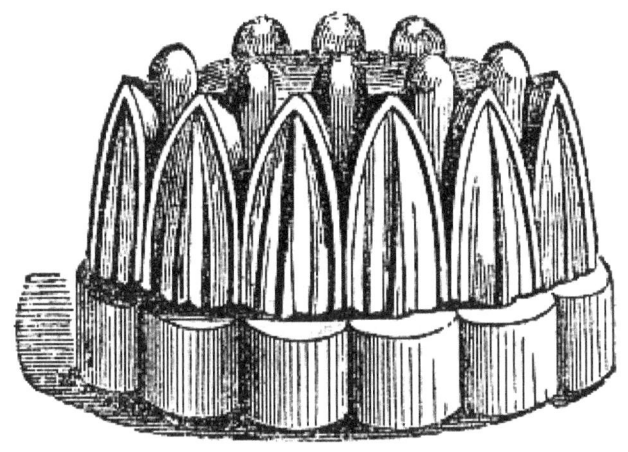
OVAL JELLY MOULD.

LIVER AND LEMON SAUCE, for Poultry.

Ingredients.—The liver of a fowl, one lemon, salt to taste, ½ pint of melted butter. *Mode.*—Wash the liver, and let it boil for a few minutes; peel the lemon very thin, remove the white part and pips, and cut it into very small dice; mince the liver and a small quantity of the lemon-rind very fine; add these ingredients to ½ pint of smoothly-made melted butter; season with a little salt, put in the cut lemon, heat it gradually, but do not allow it to boil, lest the butter should oil. *Time.*—1 minute to simmer. *Sufficient* to serve with a pair of small fowls.

LIVER AND PARSLEY SAUCE, for Poultry.

Ingredients.—The liver of a fowl, one tablespoonful of minced parsley, ½ pint of melted butter. *Mode.*—Wash and score the liver, boil it for a few minutes, and mince it very fine; blanch or scald a small bunch of parsley, of which there should be sufficient when chopped to fill a tablespoon; add this with the minced liver, to ½ pint of smoothly-made melted butter; let it just boil; when serve. *Time.*—1 minute to simmer. *Sufficient* for a pair of small fowls.

LOBSTERS, to Boil.

Ingredients.—¼ lb. of salt to each gallon of water. *Mode.*—Buy the lobsters alive, and choose those that are heavy and full of motion, which is an indication of their freshness. When the shell is incrusted, it is a sign they are old: medium-sized lobsters are the best. Have ready a stewpan of boiling water, salted in the above proportion; put in the lobster, and keep it boiling quickly from 20 minutes to ¾ hour, according to its size, and do not forget to skim well. If it boils too long, the meat becomes thready, and if not done enough, the spawn is not red: this must be obviated by great attention. Rub the shell over with a little butter or sweet oil, which wipe off again. *Time.*—Small lobster, 20 minutes to ½ hour; large ditto, ½ to ¾ hour. *Average cost*, medium size, 1*s*. 6*d*. to 2*s*. 6*d*. *Seasonable* all the year, but best from March to October.

To Choose Lobsters.—This shellfish, if it has been cooked alive, as it ought to have been, will have a stiffness in the tail, which, if gently raised, will return with a spring. Care, however, must be taken in thus proving it; for if the tail is pulled straight out, it will not return; when the fish might be pronounced inferior, which, in reality, may not be the case. In order to be good, lobsters should be weighty for their bulk; if light, they will be watery; and those of the medium size, are always the best. Small-sized lobsters are cheapest, and answer very well for sauce. In boiling lobsters, the appearance of the shell will be much improved by rubbing over it a little butter or salad-oil on being immediately taken from the pot.

LOBSTER CURRY (an Entrée).

Ingredients.—1 lobster, 2 onions, 1 oz. butter, 1 tablespoonful of curry-powder, ½ pint of medium stock, the juice of ½ lemon. *Mode.*—Pick the meat from the shell, and cut into nice square pieces; fry the onions of a pale brown in the butter, stir in the curry-powder and stock, and simmer till it thickens, when put in the lobster; stew the whole slowly for ½ hour, stirring occasionally; and just before sending to table, put in the lemon-juice. Serve boiled rice with it, the same as for other curries. *Time.*—Altogether, ¾ hour. *Average cost*, 3*s*. *Seasonable* at any time.

LOBSTER CUTLETS (an Entrée).

Ingredients.—1 large hen lobster, 1 oz. fresh butter, ½ saltspoonful of salt, pounded mace, grated nutmeg, cayenne and white pepper to taste, egg, and bread-crumbs. *Mode.*—Pick the meat from the shell, and pound it in a mortar with the butter, and gradually add the mace and seasoning, well mixing the ingredients; beat all to a smooth paste, and add a little of the spawn; divide the mixture into pieces of an equal size, and shape them like cutlets. They should not be very thick. Brush them over with egg, and sprinkle with bread-crumbs, and stick a short piece of the small claw in the top of each; fry them of a nice brown in boiling lard, and drain them before the fire, on a sieve reversed; arrange them nicely on a dish, and pour béchamel in the middle, but not over the cutlets. *Time.*—About 8 minutes after the cutlets are made. *Average cost* for this dish, 2*s*. 9*d*. *Seasonable* all the year. *Sufficient* for 5 or 6 persons.

LOBSTERS, to Dress.

When the lobster is boiled, rub it over with a little salad-oil, which wipe off again; separate the body from the tail, break off the great claws, and crack them at the joints, without injuring the meat; split the tail in halves, and arrange all neatly in a dish, with the body upright in the middle, and garnish with parsley.

LOBSTER, Hot.

Ingredients.—1 lobster, 2 oz. of butter, grated nutmeg; salt, pepper, and pounded mace, to taste; broad crumbs, 2 eggs. *Mode.*—Pound the meat of the lobster to a smooth paste with the butter and seasoning, and add a few bread-crumbs. Beat the eggs, and make the whole mixture into the form of a lobster; pound the spawn, and sprinkle over it. Bake ¼ hour, and just before serving, lay over it the tail and body shell, with the small claws underneath, to resemble a lobster. *Time.*—¼ hour. *Average cost*, 2*s*. 6*d*. *Seasonable* at any time. *Sufficient* for 4 or 5 persons.

LOBSTER PATTIES (an Entrée).

Ingredients.—Minced lobster, 4 tablespoonfuls of béchamel, 6 drops of anchovy sauce, lemon-juice, cayenne to taste. *Mode.*—Line the patty-pans with puff-paste, and put into each a small piece of bread; cover with paste, brush over with egg, and bake of a light colour. Take as much lobster as is required, mince the meat very fine, and add the above ingredients; stir it over the fire for 5 minutes; remove the lids of the patty-cases, take out the bread, fill with the mixture, and replace the covers. *Seasonably* at any time.

LOBSTER, Potted.

Ingredients.—2 lobsters; seasoning to taste, of nutmeg, pounded mace, white pepper, and salt; ¼ lb. of butter, 3 or 4 bay-leaves. *Mode.*—Take out the meat carefully from the shell, but do not cut it up. Put some butter at the bottom of a dish, lay in the lobster as evenly as possible, with the bay-leaves and seasoning between. Cover with butter, and bake for ¾ hour in a gentle oven. When done, drain the whole on a sieve, and lay the pieces in potting-jars, with the seasoning about them. When cold, pour over it clarified butter, and, if very highly seasoned, it will keep some time. *Time.*—¾ hour. *Average cost* for this quantity, 4*s.* 4*d. Seasonable* at any time.

Note.—Potted lobster may be used cold, or as a *fricassee* with cream sauce.

LOBSTER (à la Mode Française).

Ingredients.—1 lobster, 4 tablespoonfuls of white stock, 2 tablespoonfuls of cream, pounded mace, and cayenne to taste; bread-crumbs. *Mode.*—Pick the meat from the shell, and cut it up into small square pieces; put the stock, cream, and seasoning into a stewpan, add the lobster, and let it simmer gently for 6 minutes. Serve it in the shell, which must be nicely cleaned, and have a border of puff-paste; cover it with bread-crumbs, place small pieces of butter over, and brown before the fire, or with a salamander. *Time.*—¼ hour. *Average cost*, 2*s.* 6*d. Seasonable* at any time.

LOBSTER SALAD.

Ingredients.—1 hen lobster, lettuces, endive, small salad (whatever is in season), a little chopped beetroot, 2 hard-boiled eggs, a few slices of cucumber. For dressing, 4 tablespoonfuls of oil, 2 do. of vinegar, 1 teaspoonful of made mustard, the yolks of 2 eggs; cayenne and salt to taste; ¼ teaspoonful of anchovy sauce. These ingredients should be mixed perfectly smooth, and form a creamy-looking sauce. *Mode.*—Wash the salad, and thoroughly dry it by shaking it in a cloth. Cut up the lettuces and endive, pour the dressing on them, and lightly throw in the small salad. Mix all well together with the pickings from the body of the lobster; pick the meat from the shell, cut it up into nice square pieces, put half in the salad, the other half reserve for garnishing. Separate the yolks from the whites of 2 hard-boiled eggs; chop the whites very fine, and rub the yolks through a sieve, and afterwards the coral from the inside. Arrange the salad lightly on a glass dish, and garnish, first with a row of sliced cucumber, then with the pieces of lobster, the yolks and whites of the eggs, coral, and beetroot placed alternately, and arranged in small separate bunches, so that the colours contrast nicely. *Average cost*, 3*s*. 6*d*. *Sufficient* for 4 or 5 persons. *Seasonable* from April to October; may be had all the year, but salad is scarce and expensive in winter.

Note.—A few crayfish make a pretty garnishing to lobster salad.

LOBSTER SAUCE, to serve with Turbot, Salmon, Brill, &c. (very Good.)

Ingredients.—1 middling-sized hen lobster, ¾ pint of melted butter, 1 tablespoonful of anchovy sauce, ½ oz. of butter, salt and cayenne to taste, a little pounded mace when liked, 2 or 3 tablespoonfuls of cream. *Mode*.—Choose a hen lobster, as this is indispensable, in order to render this sauce as good as it ought to be. Pick the meat from the shells, and cut it into small square pieces; put the spawn, which will be found under the tail of the lobster, into a mortar with ½ oz. of butter, and pound it quite smooth; rub it through a hair-sieve, and cover up till wanted. Make ¾ pint of melted butter; put in all the ingredients except the lobster-meat, and well mix the sauce before the lobster is added to it, as it should retain its square form, and not come to table shredded and ragged. Put in the meat, let it get thoroughly hot, but do not allow it to boil, as the colour would immediately be spoiled; for it must be remembered that this sauce should always have a bright red appearance. If it is intended to be served with turbot or brill, a little of the spawn (dried and rubbed through a sieve without butter) should be saved to garnish with; but as the goodness, flavour, and appearance of the sauce so much depend on having a proper quantity of spawn, the less used for garnishing the better. *Time*.—1 minute to simmer. *Average cost*, for this quantity, 2*s*. *Seasonable* at any time. *Sufficient* to serve with a small turbot, a brill, or salmon for 6 persons.

Note.—Melted butter made with milk, will be found to answer very well for lobster sauce, as by employing it a nice white colour will be obtained.

Less quantity than the above may be made by using a very small lobster, to which add only ½ pint of melted butter, and season as above. Where economy is desired, the cream may be dispensed with, and the remains of a cold lobster left from table, may, with a little care, be converted into a very good sauce.

LOBSTER SOUP.

Ingredients.—3 large lobsters, or 6 small ones; the crumb of a French roll, 2 anchovies, 1 onion, 1 small bunch of sweet herbs, 1 strip of lemon-peel, 2 oz. of butter, a little nutmeg, 1 teaspoonful of flour, 1 pint of cream, 1 pint of milk; forcemeat balls, mace, salt, and pepper to taste, bread-crumbs, 1 egg, 2 quarts of water. *Mode.*—Pick the meat from the lobsters, and beat the fins, chine, and small claws in a mortar, previously taking away the brown fin and the bag in the head. Put it in a stewpan, with the crumb of the roll, anchovies, onions, herbs, lemon-peel, and the water; simmer gently till all the goodness is extracted, and strain it off. Pound the spawn in a mortar, with the butter, nutmeg, and flour, and mix with it the cream and milk. Give one boil up, at the same time adding the tails cut in pieces. Make the forcemeat balls with the remainder of the lobster, seasoned with mace, pepper, and salt, adding a little flour, and a few bread-crumbs; moisten them with the egg, heat them in the soup, and serve. *Time.*—2 hours, or rather more. *Average cost*, 3*s.* 6*d.* per quart. *Seasonable* from April to October. *Sufficient* for 8 persons.

LUNCHEONS.

The remains of cold joints, nicely garnished, a few sweets, or a little hashed meat, poultry or game, are the usual articles placed on the table for luncheon, with bread, and cheese, biscuits, butter, &c. If a substantial meal is desired, rump-steaks or mutton chops may be served, as also veal cutlets, kidneys, or any dish of that kind. In families where there is a nursery, the mistress of the house often partakes of the meal with the children, and makes it her luncheon. In the summer, a few dishes of fresh fruit should be added to the luncheon, or, instead of this, a compôte of fruit or fruit tart, or pudding.

MACARONI, as usually served with the CHEESE COURSE.

I.

Ingredients.—½ lb. of pipe macaroni, 1 lb. of butter, 6 oz. of Parmesan or Cheshire cheese, pepper and salt to taste, 1 pint of milk, 2 pints of water, bread-crumbs. *Mode.*—Put the milk and water into a saucepan with sufficient salt to flavour it; place it on the fire, and, when it boils quickly, drop in the macaroni. Keep the water boiling until it is quite tender; drain the macaroni, and put it into a deep dish. Have ready the grated cheese, either Parmesan or Cheshire; sprinkle it amongst the macaroni and some of the butter cut into small pieces, reserving some of the cheese for the top layer. Season with a little pepper, and cover the top layer of cheese with some very fine bread-crumbs. Warm, without oiling, the remainder of the butter, and pour it gently over the bread-crumbs, Place the dish before a bright fire to brown the crumbs; turn it once or twice, that it may be equally coloured, and serve very hot. The top of the macaroni may be browned with a salamander, which is even better than placing it before the fire, as the process is more expeditious; but it should never be browned in the oven, as the butter would oil, and so impart a very disagreeable flavour to the dish. In boiling the macaroni, let it be perfectly tender but firm, no part beginning to melt, and the form entirely preserved. It may be boiled in plain-water, with a little salt instead of using milk, but should then have a small piece of butter mixed with it. *Time.*—1 to 1½ hours to boil the macaroni, 5 minutes to brown it before the fire. *Average cost,* 1*s.* 6*d. Sufficient* for 6 or 7 persons. *Seasonable* at any time.

Note.—Riband macaroni may be dressed in the same manner, but does not require boiling so long a time.

II.

Ingredients.—¼ lb. of pipe or riband macaroni, ½ pint of milk, ½ pint of veal or beef gravy, the yolks of 2 eggs, 4 tablespoonfuls of cream, 3 oz. of grated Parmesan or Cheshire cheese, 1 oz. of butter. *Mode.*—Wash the macaroni, and boil it in the gravy and milk until quite tender, without being broken. Drain it, and put it into rather a deep dish. Beat the yolks of the eggs with the cream and 2 tablespoonfuls of the liquor the macaroni was boiled in; make this sufficiently hot to thicken, but do not allow it to boil; pour it over the macaroni, over which sprinkle the grated cheese and the butter broken into small pieces; brown with a salamander, or before the fire, and serve. *Time.*—1 to 1½ hour to boil the macaroni, 5 minutes to thicken the eggs and cream, 5 minutes to brown. *Average cost*, 1*s.* 2*d*. *Sufficient* for 3 or 4 persons, *Seasonable* at any time.

III.

Ingredients.—¼ lb. of pipe macaroni, ½ pint of brown gravy No. 436, 6 oz. of grated Parmesan cheese. *Mode.*—Wash the macaroni, and boil it in salt and water until quite tender; drain it, and put it into rather a deep dish. Have ready a pint of good brown gravy, pour it hot over the macaroni, and send it to table with grated Parmesan served on a separate dish. When the flavour is liked, a little pounded mace may be added to the water in which the macaroni is boiled; but this must always be sparingly added, as it will impart a very strong flavour. *Time.*—1 to 1½ hour to boil the macaroni. *Average cost*, with the gravy and cheese, 1*s.* 3*d*. *Sufficient* for 3 or 4 persons. *Seasonable* at any time.

MACARONI, Sweet Pudding.

Ingredients.—2½ oz. of macaroni, 2 pints, of milk, the rind of ½ lemon, 3 eggs, sugar and grated nutmeg to taste, 2 tablespoonfuls of brandy. *Mode.* —Put the macaroni, with a pint of the milk, into a saucepan with the lemon-peel, and let it simmer gently until the macaroni is tender: then put it into a pie-dish without the peel; mix the other pint of milk with the eggs; stir these well together, adding the sugar and brandy, and pour the mixture over the macaroni. Grate a little nutmeg over the top, and bake in a moderate oven for ½ hour. To make this pudding look nice, a paste should be laid round the edges of the dish, and, for variety, a layer of preserve or marmalade may be placed on the macaroni: in this case, omit the brandy. *Time.*—1 hour to simmer the macaroni; ½ hour to bake the pudding. *Average cost*, 11*d*. *Sufficient* for 5 or 6 persons. *Seasonable* at any time.

MACARONI SOUP.

Ingredients.—3 oz. of macaroni, a piece of butter the size of a walnut, salt to taste, 2 quarts of clear stock. *Mode.*—Throw the macaroni and butter into boiling water, with a pinch of salt, and simmer for ½ an hour. When it is tender, drain and cut it into thin rings or lengths, and drop it into the boiling stock. Stew gently for 15 minutes, and serve grated Parmesan cheese with it. *Time.*—¾ to 1 hour. *Average cost*, 1s. per quart. *Seasonable* all the year. *Sufficient* for 8 persons.

MACARONI, a Sweet Dish of.

Ingredients.—¼ lb. of macaroni, 1½ pint of milk, the rind of ½ lemon, 3 oz. of lump sugar, ¾ pint of custard. *Mode.*—Put the milk into a saucepan, with the lemon-peel and sugar; bring it to the boiling-point, drop in the macaroni, and let it gradually swell over a gentle fire, but do not allow the pipes to break. The form should be entirely preserved; and, though tender, should be firm, and not soft, with no part beginning to melt. Should the milk dry away before the macaroni is sufficiently swelled, add a little more. Make a custard, place the macaroni on a dish, and pour the custard over the hot macaroni; grate over it a little nutmeg, and, when cold, garnish the dish with slices of candied citron. *Time.*—From 40 to 50 minutes to swell the macaroni. *Average cost*, with the custard, 1s. *Sufficient* for 4 or 5 persons. *Seasonable* at any time.

MACAROONS.

Ingredients.—½ lb. of sweet almonds, ½ lb. of sifted loaf sugar, the whites of three eggs, wafer paper. *Mode.*—Blanch, skin and dry the almonds, and pound them well with a little orange flower or plain water, then add the sifted sugar and the whites of the eggs, which should be beaten to a stiff froth, and mix all the ingredients well together. When the paste looks soft, drop it at equal distances from a biscuit syringe on to sheets of wafer paper: put a strip of almond on the top of each; strew some syrup over, and bake the macaroons in rather a slow oven, of a light brown colour. When hard and set, they are done. They must not be allowed to get very brown, as that would spoil their appearance. If the cakes when baked, appear heavy, add a little more white of egg, which should be well whisked up before it is added to the other ingredients. *Time.*—From 15 to 20 minutes. *Average cost*, 1*s.* 8*d.* per lb.

MACKEREL.

In choosing this fish, purchasers should, to a great extent, be regulated by the brightness of its appearance. If it has a transparent, silvery hue, the flesh is good; but if it be red about the head, it is stale.

MACKEREL, Baked.

Ingredients.— 4 middling-sized mackerel, a nice delicate forcemeat, 3 oz. of butter; pepper and salt to taste. *Mode.*—Clean the fish, take out the roes, and fill up with forcemeat, and sew up the slit. Flour, and put them in a dish, heads and tails alternately, with the roes; and, between each layer, put some little pieces of butter, and pepper and salt. Bake for ½ an hour, and either serve with plain melted butter or a *maître d'hôtel* sauce. *Time.*—½ hour. *Average cost* for this quantity, 1*s.* 10*d. Seasonable* from April to July. *Sufficient* for 6 persons.

Note.—Baked mackerel may be dressed in the same way as baked herrings, and may also be stewed in wine.

MACKEREL, Boiled.

Ingredients.—¼ lb. of salt to each gallon of water. *Mode.*—Cleanse the inside of the fish thoroughly, and lay it in the kettle with sufficient water to cover it with salt as above; bring it gradually to boil, skim well, and simmer gently till done; dish them on a hot napkin, heads and tails alternately, and garnish with fennel. Fennel sauce and plain melted butter are the usual accompaniments to boiled mackerel; but caper or anchovy sauce is sometimes served with it. *Time.*—After the water boils, 10 minutes; for large mackerel, allow more time. *Average cost,* from 4*d. Seasonable* from April to July.

Note.—When variety is desired, fillet the mackerel, boil it, and pour over parsley and butter; send some of this, besides, in a tureen.

MACKEREL, Broiled.

Ingredients.—Pepper and salt to taste, a small quantity of oil. *Mode.*—Mackerel should never be washed when intended to be broiled, but merely wiped very clean and dry, after taking out the gills and insides. Open the back, and put in a little pepper, salt, and oil; broil it over a clear fire, turn it over on both sides, and also on the back. When sufficiently cooked, the flesh can be detached from the bone, which will be in about 10 minutes for a small mackerel. Chop a little parsley, work it up in the butter with pepper and salt to taste, and a squeeze of lemon-juice, and put it in the back. Serve before the butter is quite melted, with a *maître d'hôtel* sauce in a tureen. *Time.*—Small mackerel 10 minutes. *Average cost*, from 4*d*. *Seasonable* from April to July.

MACKEREL, Fillets of.

Ingredients.—2 large mackerel, 1 oz. butter, 1 small bunch of chopped herbs, 3 tablespoonfuls of medium stock, 3 tablespoonfuls of béchamel; salt, cayenne, and lemon-juice to taste. *Mode.*—Clean the fish, and fillet it; scald the herbs, chop them fine, and put them with the butter and stock into a stewpan. Lay in the mackerel, and simmer very gently for 10 minutes; take them out, and put them on a hot dish. Dredge in a little flour, add the other ingredients, give one boil, and pour it over the mackerel. *Time.*—20 minutes. *Average cost* for this quantity, 1*s*. 6*d*. *Seasonable* from April to July. *Sufficient* for 4 persons.

Note.—Fillets of mackerel may be covered with egg and bread-crumbs, and fried of a nice brown. Serve with *maître d'hôtel* sauce and plain melted butter.

MACKEREL, Pickled.

Ingredients.—12 peppercorns, 2 bay-leaves, ½ pint of vinegar, 4 mackerel. *Mode.*—Boil the mackerel, and lay them in a dish; take half the liquor they were boiled in; add as much vinegar, peppercorns, and bay-leaves; boil for 10 minutes, and when cold, pour over the fish. *Time.*—½ hour. *Average cost*, 1*s*. 6*d*.

MACKEREL, Potted.

Ingredients.—Mackerel, a blade of mace, cayenne, salt, and 2 oz. or more butter, according to the quantity of mackerel. *Mode.*—Any remains of cooked mackerel may be potted as follows; pick it well from the bones, break it into very small pieces, and put into a stewpan with the butter, pounded mace, and other ingredients; warm it thoroughly, but do not let it boil; press it into potting pots and pour clarified butter over it.

MAIGRE SOUP (i.e., Soup without Meat).

Ingredients.—6 oz. butter, 6 onions sliced, 4 heads of celery, 2 lettuces, a small bunch of parsley, 2 handfuls of spinach, 3 pieces of bread-crust, 2 blades of mace, salt and pepper to taste, the yolks of 2 eggs, 3 teaspoonfuls of vinegar, 2 quarts of water. *Mode.*—Melt the butter in a stewpan, and put in the onions to stew gently for 3 or 4 minutes; then add the celery, spinach, lettuces, and parsley, cut small. Stir the ingredients well for 10 minutes. Now put in the water, bread, seasoning, and mace. Boil gently for 1½ hour, and, at the moment of serving, beat in the yolks of the eggs and the vinegar, but do not let it boil, or the eggs will curdle. *Time.*—2 hours. *Average cost*, 6*d.* per quart. *Seasonable* all the year. *Sufficient* for 8 persons.

MAIZE, Boiled.

Ingredients.—The ears of young and green Indian wheat; to every ½ gallon of water allow 1 heaped tablespoonful of salt. *Mode.*—This vegetable, which makes one of the most delicious dishes, brought to table, is unfortunately very rarely seen in Britain; and we wonder that, in the gardens of the wealthy, it is not invariably cultivated. Our sun, it is true, possesses hardly power sufficient to ripen maize; but, with well-prepared ground, and in a favourable position, it might be sufficiently advanced by the beginning of autumn to serve as a vegetable. The outside sheath being taken off and the waving fibres removed, let the ears be placed in boiling water, where they should remain for about 25 minutes (a longer time may be necessary for larger ears than ordinary); and, when sufficiently boiled and well drained, they may be sent to table whole, and with a piece of toast underneath them. Melted butter should be served with them. *Time.*—25 to

35 minutes. *Average cost.*—Seldom bought. *Sufficient* 1 ear for each person. *Seasonable* in autumn.

MALT WINE.

Ingredients.—5 gallons of water, 28 lbs. of sugar, 6 quarts of sweet-wort, 6 quarts of tun, 3 lbs. of raisins,; ½ lb. of candy, 1 pint of brandy. *Mode.*—Boil the sugar and water together for 10 minutes; skim it well, and put the liquor into a convenient-sized pan or tub. Allow it to cool; then mix it with the sweet-wort and tun. Let it stand for 3 days, then put it into a barrel; here it will work or ferment for another three days or more; then bung up the cask, and keep it undisturbed for 2 or 3 mouths. After this, add the raisins (whole), the candy, and brandy, and, in 6 months' time, bottle the wine off. Those who do not brew, may procure the sweet-wort and tun from any brewer. Sweet-wort is the liquor that leaves the mash of malt before it is boiled with the hops; tun is the new beer after the whole of the brewing operation has been completed. *Time.*—To be boiled 10 minutes; to stand 3 days after mixing; to ferment 3 days; to remain in the cask 2 months before the raisins are added; bottle 6 months after. *Seasonable.*—Make this in March or October.

MANNA KROUP PUDDING.

Ingredients.—3 tablespoonfuls of manna kroup, 12 bitter almonds, 1 pint of milk, sugar to taste, 3 eggs. *Mode.*—Blanch and pound the almonds in a mortar; mix them with the manna kroup; pour over these a pint of boiling milk, and let them steep for about ¼ hour. When nearly cold, add sugar and the well-beaten eggs; mix all well together; put the pudding into a buttered dish, and bake for ½ hour. *Time.*—½ hour. *Average cost*, 8*d*. *Sufficient* for 4 or 5 persons. *Seasonable* at any time.

MARCH—BILLS OF FARE.

Dinner for 18 persons.

Third Course.

```
┌─────────────────────────────────────┐
│         Guinea-Fowls, larded,       │
│            removed by               │
│          Cabinet Pudding.           │
│  Apricot                   Rhubarb  │
│  Tartlets.   Wine Jelly.     Tart.  │
│                                     │
│          Vase of                    │
│  Custards. Flowers.  Jelly, in      │
│                      glasses.       │
│          Italian Cream.             │
│  Damson                  Cheesecakes│
│  Tart.                              │
│          Ducklings,                 │
│           removed by                │
│         Nesselrode Pudding.         │
└─────────────────────────────────────┘
```

Dessert and Ices.

Dinner for 12 persons.

First Course.—White soup; clear gravy soup; boiled salmon, shrimp sauce, and dressed cucumber; baked mullets in paper cases. *Entrées.*—Filet de bœuf and Spanish sauce; larded sweetbreads; rissoles; chicken patties. *Second Course.*—Roast fillet of veal and Béchamel sauce; boiled leg of lamb; roast fowls, garnished with water-cresses; boiled ham, garnished with carrots and mashed turnips; vegetables—sea-kale, spinach, or brocoli. *Third Course.*—Two ducklings; guinea-fowl, larded; orange jelly; Charlotte Russe; coffee cream; ice pudding; macaroni with Parmesan cheese; spinach, garnished with croûtons; dessert and ices.

Dinner for 10 persons.

First Course.—Macaroni soup; boiled turbot and lobster sauce; salmon cutlets. *Entrées.*—Compôte of pigeons; mutton cutlets and tomato sauce. *Second Course.*—Roast lamb; boiled half calf's head, tongue, and brains; boiled bacon-cheek, garnished with spoonsfuls of spinach; vegetables. *Third Course.*—Ducklings; plum-pudding; ginger cream; trifle; rhubarb tart; cheesecakes; fondues, in cases; dessert and ices.

Dinner for 8 persons.

First Course.—Calf's-head soup; brill and shrimp sauce; broiled mackerel à la Maître d'Hôtel. *Entrées.*—Lobster cutlets; calf's liver and bacon, aux fines herbes. *Second Course.*—Roast loin of veal; two boiled fowls à la Béchamel; boiled knuckle of ham; vegetables—spinach or brocoli. *Third Course.*—Wild ducks; apple custards; blancmange; lemon jelly; jam sandwiches; ice pudding; potatoes à la Maître d'Hôtel; dessert and ices.

Dinner for 6 persons.

First Course.—Vermicelli soup; soles à la Crême. *Entrées.*—Veal cutlets; small vols-au-vent. *Second Course.*—Small saddle of mutton; half calf's head; boiled bacon-cheek, garnished with Brussels sprouts. *Third Course.*—Cabinet pudding; orange jelly; custards, in glasses; rhubarb tart; lobster salad; dessert.

First Course.—Julienne soup; baked mullets. *Entrées.*—Chicken cutlets; oyster patties. *Second Course.*—Roast lamb and mint sauce; boiled leg of pork; pease pudding; vegetables. *Third Course.*—Ducklings; Swiss cream; lemon jelly; cheesecakes; rhubarb tart; macaroni; dessert.

First Course.—Oyster soup; boiled salmon and dressed cucumber. *Entrées.*—Rissoles; fricasseed chicken. *Second Course.*—Boiled leg of mutton, caper sauce; roast fowls, garnished with water-cresses; vegetables. *Third Course.*—Charlotte aux pommes; orange jelly; lemon cream; soufflé of arrowroot; sea-kale; dessert.

First Course.—Ox-tail soup; boiled mackerel. *Entrées.*—Stewed mutton kidneys; minced veal and oysters. *Second Course.*—Stewed shoulder of veal; roast ribs of beef and horseradish sauce; vegetables. *Third Course.*—Ducklings; tartlets of strawberry jam; cheesecakes; Gâteau de Riz; carrot pudding; sea-kale; dessert.

MARCH, Plain Family Dinners for.

Sunday.—1. Boiled ½ calf's head, pickled pork, the tongue on a small dish with the brains round it; mutton cutlets and mashed potatoes. 2. Plum tart made with bottled fruit, baked custard pudding, Baroness pudding.

Monday.—1. Roast shoulder of mutton and onion sauce, brocoli, baked potatoes. 2. Slices of Baroness pudding warmed, and served with sugar sprinkled over Cheesecakes.

Tuesday.—1. Mock turtle soup, made with liquor that calf's head was boiled in, and the pieces of head. 2. Hashed mutton, rump-steaks and oyster sauce. 3. Boiled plum-pudding.

Wednesday.—1. Fried whitings, melted butter, potatoes. 2. Boiled beef, suet dumplings, carrots, potatoes, marrow-bones. 3. Arrowroot blancmange, and stewed rhubarb.

Thursday.—1. Pea-soup made from liquor that beef was boiled in. 2. Stewed rump-steak, cold beef, mashed potatoes. 3. Rolled jam pudding.

Friday.—1. Fried soles, melted butter, potatoes. 2. Roast loin of mutton, brocoli, potatoes, bubble-and-squeak. 3. Rice pudding.

Saturday.—1. Rump-steak pie, haricot mutton made with remains of cold loin. 2. Pancakes, ratafia pudding.

Sunday.—1. Roast fillet of veal, boiled ham, spinach and potatoes. 2. Rhubarb tart, custards in glasses, bread-and-butter pudding.

Monday.—1. Baked soles, potatoes. 2. Minced veal and rump-steak pie. 3. Somersetshire dumplings with the remains of custards poured round them; marmalade tartlets.

Tuesday.—1. Gravy soup. 2. Boiled leg of mutton, mashed turnips, suet dumplings, caper sauce, potatoes, veal rissoles made with remains of fillet of veal. 3. Cheese.

Wednesday.—1. Stewed mullet. 2. Roast fowls, bacon, gravy, and bread sauce, mutton pudding, made with a few slices of the cold meat and the addition of two kidneys. 3. Baked lemon pudding.

Thursday.—1. Vegetable soup made with liquor that the mutton was boiled in, and mixed with the remains of gravy soup. 2. Roast ribs of beef, Yorkshire pudding, horseradish sauce, brocoli and potatoes. 3. Apple pudding or macaroni.

Friday.—1. Stewed eels, pork cutlets, and tomato sauce. 2. Cold beef, mashed potatoes. 3. Plum tart made with bottled fruit.

Saturday.—1. Rump-steak-and-kidney pudding, broiled beef-bones, greens and potatoes. 2. Jam tartlets made with pieces of paste from plum tart, baked custard pudding.

MARCH, Things in Season.

Fish.—Barbel, brill, carp, crabs, crayfish, dace, eels, flounders, haddocks, herrings, lampreys, lobsters, mussels, oysters, perch, pike, plaice, prawns, shrimps, skate, smelts, soles, sprats, sturgeon, tench, thornback, turbot, whiting.

Meat.—Beef, house lamb, mutton, pork, veal.

Poultry.—Capons, chickens, ducklings, tame and wild pigeons, pullets with eggs, turkeys, wild-fowl, though now not in full season.

Game.—Grouse, hares, partridges, pheasants, snipes, woodcock.

Vegetables.—Beetroot, brocoli (purple and white), Brussels sprouts, cabbages, carrots, celery, chervil, cresses, cucumbers (forced), endive, kidney-beans, lettuces, parsnips, potatoes, savoys, sea-kale, spinach, turnips,—various herbs.

Fruit.—Apples (golden and Dutch pippins), grapes, medlars, nuts, oranges, pears (Bon Chrétien), walnuts, dried fruits (foreign), such as almonds and raisins; French and Spanish plums; prunes, figs, dates, crystallized preserves.

MARMALADE AND VERMICELLI PUDDING.

Ingredients.—1 breakfast-cupful of vermicelli, 2 tablespoonfuls of marmalade, ¼ lb. of raisins, sugar to taste, 3 eggs, milk. *Mode.*—Pour some boiling milk on the vermicelli, and let it remain covered for 10 minutes; then mix with it the marmalade, stoned raisins, sugar, and beaten eggs. Stir all well together, put the mixture into a buttered mould, boil for 1½ hour, and serve with custard sauce. *Time.*—1½ hour. *Average cost,* 1s. *Sufficient* for 5 or 6 persons. *Seasonable* at any time.

MARROW-BONES, Boiled.

Ingredients.—Bones, a small piece of common paste, a floured cloth. *Mode.*—Have the bones neatly sawed into convenient sizes, and cover the ends with a small piece of common crust, made with flour and water. Over this tie a floured cloth, and place the bones upright in a saucepan of boiling water, taking care there is sufficient to cover them. Boil them for 2 hours, remove the cloth and paste, and serve them upright on a napkin with dry toast. Many persons clear the marrow from the bones after they are cooked, spread it over a slice of toast and add a seasoning of pepper: when served in this manner, it must be very expeditiously sent to table, as it so soon gets cold. *Time.*—2 hours. *Seasonable* at any time.

Note.—Marrow-bones may be baked after preparing them as in the preceding recipe; they should be laid in a deep dish, and baked for 2 hours.

MARROW DUMPLINGS, to serve with Roast Meat, in Soup, with Salad, &c.
(*German Recipe.*)

Ingredients.—1 oz. of beef marrow, 1 oz. of butter, 2 eggs, 2 penny rolls, 1 teaspoonful of minced onion, 1 teaspoonful of minced parsley, salt and grated nutmeg to taste. *Mode.*—Beat the marrow and butter together to a cream; well whisk the eggs, and add these to the other ingredients. When they are well stirred, put in the rolls, which should previously be well soaked in boiling milk, strained, and beaten up with a fork. Add the remaining ingredients, omitting the minced onion where the flavour is very much disliked, and form the mixture into small round dumplings. Drop these into boiling broth, and let them simmer for about 20 minutes or ½ hour. They may be served in soup, with roast meat, or with salad, as in Germany, where they are more frequently sent to table than in this country. They are very good. *Time.*—20 minutes to ½ hour. *Average cost,* 6*d.* *Sufficient* for 7 or 8 dumplings. *Seasonable* at any time.

MARROW PUDDING, Baked or Boiled.

Ingredients.—½ pint of bread-crumbs, 1½ pint of milk, 6 oz. of marrow, 4 eggs, ¼ lb. of raisins or currants, or 2 oz. of each; sugar and grated nutmeg to taste. *Mode.*—Make the milk boiling, pour it hot on to the bread-crumbs, and let these remain covered for about ½ hour; shred the marrow, beat up the eggs, and mix these with the bread-crumbs; add the remaining ingredients, beat the mixture well, and either put it into a buttered mould and boil it for 2½ hours, or put it into a pie-dish edged with puff-paste, and bake for rather more than ¾ hour. Before sending it to table, sift a little pounded sugar over, after being turned out of the mould or basin. *Time.*—2½ hours to boil, ¾ hour to bake. *Average cost,* 1*s.* 2*d.* *Sufficient* for 5 or 6 persons. *Seasonable* at any time.

MAY—BILLS OF FARE.

Dinner for 18 persons.

First Course.

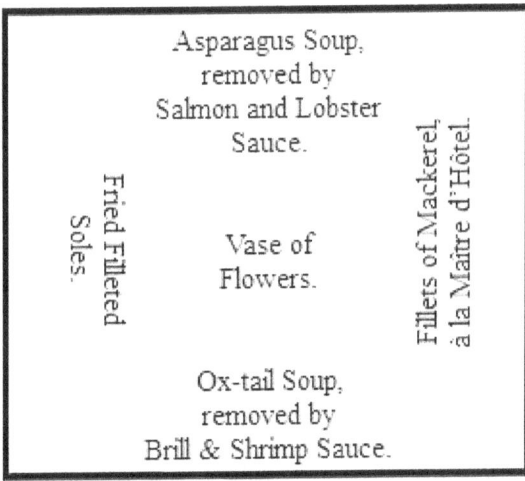

Entrées.

Dinner for 12 persons.

First Course.—White soup; asparagus soup; salmon cutlets; boiled turbot and lobster sauce. *Entrées.*—Chicken vol-au-vent; lamb cutlets and cucumbers; fricandeau of veal; stewed mushrooms. *Second Course.*—Roast lamb; haunch of mutton; boiled and roast fowls; vegetables. *Third Course.*—Ducklings; goslings; Charlotte Russe; Vanilla cream; gooseberry tart; custards; cheesecakes; cabinet pudding and iced pudding; dessert and ices.

Dinner for 10 persons.

First Course.—Spring soup; salmon à la Genévése; red mullet. *Entrées.*—Chicken vol-au-vent; calf's liver and bacon aux fines herbes. *Second Course.*—Saddle of mutton; half calf's head, tongue, and brains; braised ham; asparagus. *Third Course.*—Roast pigeons; ducklings; sponge-cake pudding; Charlotte à la vanille; gooseberry tart; cream; cheesecakes; apricot-jam tart; dessert and ices.

Dinner for 8 persons.

First Course.—Julienne soup; brill and lobster sauce; fried fillets of mackerel. *Entrées.*—Lamb cutlets and cucumbers; lobster patties. *Second Course.*—Roast fillet of veal; boiled leg of lamb; asparagus. *Third Course.*—Ducklings; gooseberry tart; custards; fancy pastry; soufflé; dessert and ices.

Dinner for 6 persons.

First Course.—Vermicelli soup; boiled salmon and anchovy sauce. *Entrées.*—Fillets of beef and tomato sauce; sweetbreads. *Second Course.*—Roast lamb; boiled capon; asparagus. *Third Course.*—Ducklings; cabinet pudding; compôte of gooseberries; custards in glasses; blancmange; lemon tartlets; fondue; dessert.

First Course.—Macaroni soup; boiled mackerel à la maître d'hôtel; fried smelts. *Entrées.*—Scollops of fowl; lobster pudding. *Second Course.*—Boiled leg of lamb and spinach; roast sirloin of beef and horseradish sauce; vegetables. *Third Course.*—Roast leveret; salad; soufflé of rice; ramakins; strawberry-jam tartlets; orange jelly; dessert.

First Course.—Julienne soup; trout with Dutch sauce; salmon cutlets. *Entrées.*—Lamb cutlets and mushrooms; vol-au-vent of chicken. *Second Course.*—Roast lamb; calf's head à la tortue; vegetables. *Third Course.*—Spring chickens; iced pudding; Vanilla cream; clear jelly; tartlets; cheesecakes; dessert.

First Course.—Soup à la reine; crimped trout and lobster sauce; baked whitings aux fines herbes. *Entrées.*—Braised mutton cutlets and cucumbers; stewed pigeons. *Second Course.*—Roast fillet of veal; bacon-cheek and greens; fillet of beef à la jardinière. *Third Course.*—Ducklings; soufflé à la vanille; compôte of oranges; meringues; gooseberry tart; fondue; dessert.

MAY, Plain Family Dinners for.

Sunday.—1. Vegetable soup. 2. Saddle of mutton, asparagus and potatoes. 3. Gooseberry tart, custards.

Monday.—1. Fried whitings, anchovy sauce. 2. Cold mutton, mashed potatoes, stewed veal. 3. Fig pudding.

Tuesday.—1. Haricot mutton, made from remains of cold mutton, rump-steak pie. 2. Macaroni.

Wednesday.—1. Roast loin of veal and spinach, boiled bacon, mutton cutlets and tomato sauce. 2. Gooseberry pudding and cream.

Thursday.—1. Spring soup. 2. Roast leg of lamb, mint sauce, spinach, curried veal and rice. 3. Lemon pudding.

Friday.—1. Boiled mackerel and parsley-and-butter. 2. Stewed rump-steak, cold lamb and salad. 3. Baked gooseberry pudding.

Saturday.—1. Vermicelli. 2. Rump-steak pudding, lamb cutlets, and cucumbers. 3. Macaroni.

Sunday.—1. Boiled salmon and lobster or caper sauce. 2. Roast lamb, mint sauce, asparagus, potatoes. 3. Plum-pudding, gooseberry tart.

Monday.—1. Salmon warmed in remains of lobster sauce and garnished with croûtons. 2. Stewed knuckle of veal and rice, cold lamb and dressed cucumber. 3. Slices of pudding warmed, and served with sugar sprinkled over. Baked rice pudding.

Tuesday.—1. Roast ribs of beef, horseradish sauce, Yorkshire pudding, spinach and potatoes. 2. Boiled lemon pudding.

Wednesday.—1. Fried soles, melted butter. 2. Cold beef and dressed cucumber or salad, veal cutlets and bacon. 3. Baked plum-pudding.

Thursday.—1. Spring soup. 2. Calf's liver and bacon, broiled beef-bones, spinach and potatoes. 3. Gooseberry tart.

Friday.—1. Roast shoulder of mutton, baked potatoes, onion sauce, spinach. 2. Currant dumplings.

Saturday.—1. Broiled mackerel, fennel sauce or plain melted butter. 2. Rump-steak pie, hashed mutton, vegetables. 3. Baked arrowroot pudding.

MAY, Things in Season.

Fish.—Carp, chub, crabs, crayfish, dory, herrings, lobsters, mackerel, red and gray mullet, prawns, salmon, shad, smelts, soles, trout, turbot.

Meat.—Beef, lamb, mutton, veal.

Poultry.—Chickens, ducklings, fowls, green geese, leverets, pullets, rabbits.

Vegetables.—Asparagus, beans, early cabbages, carrots, cauliflowers, cresses, cucumbers, lettuces, pease, early potatoes, salads, sea-kale,—various herbs.

Fruit.—Apples, green apricots, cherries, currants for tarts, gooseberries, melons, pears, rhubarb, strawberries.

MAYONNAISE, a Sauce or Salad-Dressing for cold Chicken, Meat, and other cold Dishes.

Ingredients.—The yolks of 2 eggs, 6 tablespoonfuls of salad oil, 4 tablespoonfuls of vinegar, salt and white pepper to taste, 1 tablespoonful of white stock, 2 tablespoonfuls of cream. *Mode.*—Put the yolks of the eggs into a basin, with a seasoning of pepper and salt; have ready the above quantities of oil and vinegar, in separate vessels; add them *very gradually* to the eggs; continue stirring and rubbing the mixture with a wooden spoon, as herein consists the secret of having a nice smooth sauce. It cannot be stirred too frequently, and it should be made in a very cool place, or, if ice is at hand, it should be mixed over it. When the vinegar and oil are well incorporated with the eggs, add the stock and cream, stirring all the time, and it will then be ready for use.

For a fish Mayonnaise, this sauce may be coloured with lobster-spawn, pounded; and for poultry or meat, where variety is desired, a little parsley-juice may be used to add to its appearance. Cucumber, tarragon, or any other flavoured vinegar, may be substituted for plain, where they are liked. *Average cost*, for this quantity, 7d. *Sufficient* for a small salad.

Note.—In mixing the oil and vinegar with the eggs, put in first a few drops of oil, and then a few drops of vinegar, never adding a large quantity of either at one time. By this means, you can be more certain of the sauce not curdling. Patience and practice, let us add, are two essentials for making this sauce good.

MELONS.

This fruit is rarely preserved or cooked in any way, but is sent whole to table on a dish garnished with leaves or flowers, as fancy dictates. A border of any other kind of small fruit, arranged round the melon, has a pretty effect, the colour of the former contrasting nicely with the melon. Plenty of pounded sugar should be served with it; and the fruit should be cut lengthwise, in moderate-sized slices. In America, it is frequently eaten with pepper and salt. *Average cost.*—English, in full season, 3*s.* 6*d.* to 5*s.* each; when scarce, 10*s.* to 15*s.*; *seasonable*, June to August. French, 2*s.* to 3*s.* 6*d.* each; *seasonable*, June and July. Dutch, 9*d.* to 2*s.* each; *seasonable*, July and August.

MERINGUES.

MERINGUES.

Ingredients.—½ lb. of pounded sugar, the whites of 4 eggs. *Mode.*—Whisk the whites of the eggs to a stiff froth, and, with a wooden spoon, stir in *quickly* the pounded sugar; and have some boards thick enough to put in the oven to prevent the bottom of the meringues from acquiring too much colour. Cut some strips of paper about 2 inches wide; place this paper on the board, and drop a tablespoonful at a time of the mixture on the paper, taking care to let all the meringues be the same size. In dropping it from the spoon, give the mixture the form of an egg, and keep the meringues about 2 inches apart from each other on the paper. Strew over them some sifted sugar, and bake in a moderate oven for ½ hour. As soon as they begin to colour, remove them from the oven; take each slip of paper by the two ends, and turn it gently on the table, and, with a small spoon, take out the soft part of each meringue. Spread some clean paper on the board, turn the meringues upside down, and put them into the oven to harden and brown on the other side. When required for table, fill them with whipped cream, flavoured with liqueur or vanilla, and sweetened with pounded sugar. Join two of the meringues together, and pile them high in the dish, as shown in the annexed drawing. To vary their appearance, finely-chopped almonds or currants may be strewn over them before the sugar is sprinkled over; and they may be garnished with any bright-coloured preserve. Great expedition is necessary in making this sweet dish; as, if the meringues are not put into the oven as soon as the sugar and eggs are mixed, the former melts, and the mixture would run on the paper, instead of keeping its egg-shape. The sweeter the meringues are made, the crisper will they be; but, if there is not sufficient sugar mixed with them, they will most likely be tough. They are sometimes coloured with cochineal; and, if kept well covered in a dry place, will remain good for a month or six weeks. *Time.*—Altogether, about ½ hour. *Average cost*, with the cream and flavouring, 1*s*. *Sufficient* to make 2 dozen meringues. *Seasonable* at any time.

MILK.

Milk, when of good quality, is of an opaque white colour: the cream always comes to the top; the well-known milky odour is strong; it will boil without altering its appearance in these respects; the little bladders which arise on the surface will renew themselves if broken by the spoon. To boil milk is, in fact, the simplest way of testing its quality. The commonest adulterations of milk are not of a hurtful character. It is a good deal thinned with water, and sometimes thickened with a little starch, or coloured with yolk of egg, or even saffron; but these processes have nothing murderous in them.

MILK AND CREAM, to keep, in hot Weather.

When the weather is very warm, and it is very difficult to prevent milk from turning sour and spoiling the cream, it should be scalded, and it will then remain good for a few hours. It must on no account be allowed to boil, or there will be a skin instead of a cream upon the milk; and the slower the process the safer will it be. A very good plan to scald milk, is to put the pan that contains it into a saucepan or wide kettle of boiling water. When the surface looks thick, the milk is sufficiently scalded, and it should then be put away in a cool place in the same vessel that it was scalded in. Cream may be kept for 24 hours, if scalded without sugar; and by the addition of the latter ingredient, it will remain good double the time, if kept in a cool place. All pans, jugs, and vessels intended for milk, should be kept beautifully clean, and well scalded before the milk is put in, as any negligence in this respect may cause large quantities of it to be spoiled; and milk should never be kept in vessels of zinc or copper. Milk may be preserved good in hot weather, for a few hours, by placing the jug which contains it in ice, or very cold water; or a pinch of bicarbonate of soda may be introduced into the liquid.

MILK AND CREAM, Separation of.

If it be desired that the milk should be freed entirely from cream, it should be poured into a very shallow broad pan or dish, not more than 1½ inch deep, as cream cannot rise through a great depth of milk. In cold and wet weather, milk is not so rich as it is in summer and warm weather, and the morning's milk is always richer than the evening's. The last-drawn milk of each milking, at all times and seasons, is richer than the first-drawn, and on that account should be set apart for cream. Milk should be shaken as little as possible when carried from the cow to the dairy, and should be poured into the pans very gently. Persons not keeping cows, may always have a little cream, provided the milk they purchase be pure and unadulterated. As soon as it comes in, it should be poured into very shallow open pie-dishes, and set by in a very cool place, and in 7 or 8 hours a nice cream should have risen to the surface.

MILK AND CREAM, Substitute for, in Tea and Coffee.

Ingredients.—1 new laid egg to every large breakfast-cupful of tea or coffee. *Mode.*—Beat up the whole of the egg in a basin, put it into a cup, and pour over it the tea or coffee quite hot, stirring all the time to prevent the egg from curdling. In point of nourishment, both tea and coffee are much improved by this addition. *Sufficient.*—1 egg to every large breakfast-cupful of tea or coffee.

MILK SOUP (a nice Dish for Children).

Ingredients.—2 quarts of milk, 1 saltspoonful of salt, 1 teaspoonful of powdered cinnamon, 3 teaspoonfuls of pounded sugar, or more if liked, 4 thin slices of bread, the yolks of 6 eggs. *Mode.*—Boil the milk with the salt, cinnamon, and sugar; lay the bread in a deep dish, pour over it a little of the milk, and keep it hot over a stove, without burning. Beat up the yolks of the eggs, add them to the milk, and stir it over the fire till it thickens. Do not let it curdle. Pour it upon the bread, and serve. *Time.*—¾ of an hour. *Average cost*, 8*d.* per quart. *Seasonable* all the year. *Sufficient* for 10 children.

MINCE PIES.

Ingredients.—Good puff-paste, mincemeat. *Mode.*—Make some good puff-paste by recipe; roll it out to the thickness of about ¼ inch, and line some good-sized patty-pans with it; fill them with mincemeat, cover with the paste, and cut it off all round close to the edge of the tin. Put the pies into a brisk oven, to draw the paste up, and bake for 25 minutes, or longer, should the pies be very large; brush them over with the white of an egg, beaten with the blade of a knife to a stiff froth; sprinkle over pounded sugar, and put them into the oven for a minute or two, to dry the egg; dish the pies on a white d'oyley, and serve hot. They may be merely sprinkled with pounded sugar instead of being glazed, when that mode is preferred. To re-warm them, put the pies on the patty-pans, and let them remain in the oven for 10 minutes or ¼ hour, and they will be almost as good as if freshly made. *Time.*—25 to 30 minutes; 10 minutes to re-warm them. *Average cost*, 4*d.* each. *Sufficient*—½ lb. of paste for 4 pies. *Seasonable* at Christmas time.

MINCE PIES.

MINCEMEAT.

Ingredients.—2 lbs. of raisins, 3 lbs. of currants, 1½ lb. of lean beef, 3 lbs. of beef suet, 2 lbs. of moist sugar, 2 oz. of citron, 2 oz. of candied lemon-peel, 2 oz. of candied orange-peel, 1 large nutmeg, 1 pottle of apples, the rind of 2 lemons, the juice of 1, ½ pint of brandy. *Mode.*—Stone and *cut* the raisins once or twice across, but do not chop them; wash, dry, and pick the currants free from stalks and grit, and mince the beef and suet, taking care that the latter is chopped very fine; slice the citron and candied peel, grate the nutmeg, and pare, core, and mince the apples; mince the lemon-peel, strain the juice, and when all the ingredients are thus prepared, mix them well together, adding the brandy when the other things are well blended; press the whole into a jar, carefully exclude the air, and the mincemeat will be ready for use in a fortnight. If an additional quantity of spice be preferred, add ½ teaspoonful of pounded mace, and the same of pounded allspice. We, however, prefer the mincemeat without the latter ingredients, and can vouch for its excellence. *Average cost* for this quantity, 8*s*. *Seasonable.*—Make this about the beginning of December.

MINCEMEAT, Excellent.

Ingredients.—3 large lemons, 3 large apples, 1 lb. of stoned raisins, 1 lb. of currants, 1 lb. of suet, 2 lbs. of moist sugar, 1 oz. of sliced candied citron, 1 oz. of sliced candied orange-peel, and the same quantity of lemon-peel, 1 teacupful of brandy, 2 tablespoonfuls of orange marmalade. *Mode.*—Grate the rinds of the lemons; squeeze out the juice, strain it, and boil the remainder of the lemons until tender enough to pulp or chop very finely. Then add to this pulp the apples, which should be baked, and their skins and cores removed; put in the remaining ingredients one by one, and, as they are added, mix everything very thoroughly together. Put the mincemeat into a stone jar with a closely-fitting lid, and in a fortnight it will be ready for use. *Seasonable.*—This should be made the first or second week in December.

MINT SAUCE, to serve with Roast Lamb.

Ingredients.—4 dessertspoonfuls of chopped mint, 2 dessertspoonfuls of pounded white sugar, ¼ pint of vinegar. *Mode.*—Wash the mint, which should be young and fresh-gathered, free from grit; pick the leaves from the stalks, mince them very fine, and put them into a tureen; add the sugar and vinegar, and stir till the former is dissolved. This sauce is better by being made 2 or 3 hours before wanted for table, as the vinegar then becomes impregnated with the flavour of the mint. By many persons, the above proportion of sugar would not be considered sufficient; but as tastes vary, we have given the quantity which we have found to suit the general palate. *Average cost*, 3*d*. *Sufficient* to serve with a middling-size joint of lamb.

Note.—Where green mint is scarce and not obtainable, mint vinegar may be substituted for it, and will be found very acceptable in early spring.

MINT VINEGAR.

Ingredients.—Vinegar, mint. *Mode.*—Procure some nice fresh mint, pick the leaves from the stalks, and fill a bottle or jar with them. Add vinegar to them until the bottle is full; *cover closely* to exclude the air, and let it infuse for a fortnight. Then strain the liquor, and put it into small bottles for use, of which the corks should be sealed. *Seasonable.*—This should be made in June, July or August.

MOCK TURTLE SOUP.

I.

Ingredients.—½ a calf's head, ¼ lb. of butter, ¼ lb. of lean ham, 2 tablespoonfuls of minced parsley, a little minced lemon thyme, sweet marjoram, basil, 2 onions, a few chopped mushrooms (when obtainable), 2 shalots, 2 tablespoonfuls of flour, ¼ bottle of Madeira or sherry, forcemeat balls, cayenne, salt and mace to taste, the juice of 1 lemon and 1 Seville orange, 1 dessertspoonful of pounded sugar, 3 quarts of best stock. *Mode.*—Scald the head with the skin on, remove the brain, tie the head up in a cloth, and let it boil for 1 hour. Then take the meat from the bones, cut it into small square pieces, and throw them into cold water. Now take the meat, put it into a stewpan, and cover with stock; let it boil gently for an hour, or rather more, if not quite tender, and set it on one side. Melt the butter in another stewpan, and add the ham, cut small, with the herbs, parsley, onions, shalots, mushrooms, and nearly a pint of stock; let these simmer slowly for 2 hours, and then dredge in as much flour as will dry up the butter. Fill up with the remainder of the stock, add the wine, let it stew gently for 10 minutes, rub it through a tammy, and put it to the calf's head; season with cayenne, and, if required, a little salt; add the juice of the orange and lemon; and when liked, ¼ teaspoonful of pounded mace, and the sugar. Put in the forcemeat balls, simmer 5 minutes, and serve very hot. *Time.*—4½ hours. *Average cost*, 3*s*. 6*d*. per quart, or 2*s*. 6*d*. without wine or forcemeat balls. *Seasonable* in winter. *Sufficient* for 10 persons.

Note.—The bones of the head should be well stewed in the liquor it was first boiled in, and will make good white stock, flavoured with vegetables, &c.

II.
(*More Economical.*)

Ingredients.—A knuckle of veal weighing 5 or 6 lbs., 2 cow-heels, 2 large onions stuck with cloves, 1 bunch of sweet herbs, 3 blades of mace, salt to taste, 12 peppercorns, 1 glass of sherry, 24 forcemeat balls, a little lemon-juice, 4 quarts of water. *Mode.*—Put all the ingredients, except the forcemeat balls and lemon-juice, in an earthen jar, and stew for 6 hours. Do not open it till cold. When wanted for use, skim off all the fat, and strain carefully; place it on the fire, cut up the meat into inch-and-a-half squares, put it, with the forcemeat balls and lemon-juice, into the soup, and serve. It can be flavoured with a tablespoonful of anchovy, or Harvey's sauce. *Time.* —6 hours. *Average cost*, 1*s*. 4*d*. per quart. *Seasonable* in winter. *Sufficient* for 10 persons.

MUFFINS.

Ingredients.—To every quart of milk allow 1½ oz. of German yeast, a little salt; flour. *Mode.*—Warm the milk, add to it the yeast, and mix these well together; put them into a pan, and stir in sufficient flour to make the whole into a dough of rather a soft consistence; cover it over with a cloth, and place it in a warm place to rise, and, when light and nicely risen, divide the dough into pieces, and round them to the proper shape with the hands; place them in a layer of flour about two inches thick, on wooden trays, and let them rise again: when this is effected, they each will exhibit a semi-globular shape. Then place them carefully on a hot plate or stove, and bake them until they are slightly browned, turning them when they are done on one side. Muffins are not easily made, and are more generally purchased than manufactured at home. *To toast them,* divide the edge of the muffin all round, by pulling it open to the depth of about an inch, with the fingers. Put it on a toasting-fork, and hold it before a very clear fire until one side is nicely browned, but not burnt; turn, and toast it on the other. Do not toast them too quickly, as, if this be done, the middle of the muffin will not be warmed through. When done, divide them by pulling them open; butter them slightly on both sides, put them together again, and cut them into halves: when sufficient are toasted and buttered, pile them on a very hot dish, and send them very quickly to table. *Time.*—From 20 minutes to ½ hour to bake them. *Sufficient.*—Allow 1 muffin to each person.

MUFFINS.

MULBERRIES, Preserved.

Ingredients.—To 2 lbs. of fruit and 1 pint of juice allow 2½ lbs. of loaf sugar. *Mode.*—Put some of the fruit into a preserving pan, and simmer it gently until the juice is well drawn. Strain it through a bag, measure it, and to every pint allow the above proportion of sugar and fruit. Put the sugar into the preserving-pan, moisten it with the juice, boil it up, skim well, and then add the mulberries, which should be ripe, but not soft enough to break to a pulp. Let them stand in the syrup till warm through, then set them on the fire to boil gently; when half done, turn them carefully into an earthen pan, and let them remain till the next day; then boil them as before, and when the syrup is thick, and becomes firm when cold, put the preserve into pots. In making this, care should be taken not to break the mulberries: this may be avoided by very gentle stirring, and by simmering the fruit very slowly. *Time.*—¾ hour to extract the juice; ¼ hour to boil the mulberries the first time, ¼ hour the second time. *Seasonable* in August and September.

MULLAGATAWNY SOUP.

Ingredients.—2 tablespoonfuls of curry powder, 6 onions, 1 clove of garlic, 1 oz. of pounded almonds, a little lemon-pickle, or mango-juice, to taste; 1 fowl or rabbit; 4 slices of lean bacon; 2 quarts of medium stock, or, if wanted very good, best stock. *Mode.*—Slice and fry the onions of a nice colour; line the stewpan with the bacon; cut up the rabbit or fowl into small joints, and slightly brown them; put in the fried onions, the garlic, and stock and simmer gently till the meat is tender, skim very carefully, and when the meat is done, rub the curry powder to a smooth batter: add it to the soup with the almonds, which must be first pounded with a little of the stock. Put in seasoning and lemon-pickle or mango-juice to taste, and serve boiled rice with it. *Time.*—2 hours. *Average cost,* 1*s.* 6*d.* per quart. *Seasonable* in winter. *Sufficient* for 8 persons.

Note.—This soup can also be made with breast of veal, or calf's head. Vegetable mullagatawny is made with veal stock, by boiling and pulping chopped vegetable marrow, cucumbers, onions, and tomatoes, and seasoning with curry powder and cayenne. Nice pieces of meat, good curry powder, and strong stock, are necessary to make this soup good.

MULLET, Grey.

Ingredients.—¼ lb. of salt to each gallon of water. *Mode.*—If the fish be very large, it should be laid in cold water, and gradually brought to a boil; if small, put it in boiling water, salted in the above proportion. Serve with anchovy sauce and plain melted butter. *Time.*—According to size, ¼ to ¾ hour. *Average cost,* 8*d.* per lb. *Seasonable* from July to October.

MULLET, Red.

Ingredients.—Oiled paper, thickening of butter and flour, ½ teaspoonful of anchovy sauce, 1 glass of sherry; cayenne and salt to taste. *Mode.*—Clean the fish, take out the gills, but leave the inside, fold in oiled paper, and bake them gently. When done, take the liquor that flows from the fish, add a thickening of butter kneaded with flour; put in the other ingredients, and let it boil for 2 minutes. Serve the sauce in a tureen, and the fish, either with or without the paper cases. *Time.*—About 25 minutes. *Average cost,* 1*s.* each. *Seasonable* at any time, but more plentiful in summer.

Note.—Red mullet may be broiled, and should be folded in oiled paper, the same as in the preceding recipe, and seasoned with pepper and salt. They may be served without sauce; but if any is required, use melted butter, Italian or anchovy sauce. They should never be plain boiled.

MUSHROOM KETCHUP.

Ingredients.—To each peck of mushrooms ½ lb. of salt; to each quart of mushroom-liquor ¼ oz. of cayenne, ½ oz. of allspice, ½ oz. of ginger, 2 blades of pounded mace. *Mode.*—Choose full-grown mushroom flaps, and take care they are perfectly *fresh gathered* when the weather is tolerably dry; for, if they are picked during very heavy rain, the ketchup from which they are made is liable to get musty, and will not keep long. Put a layer of them in a deep pan, sprinkle salt over them, and then another layer of mushrooms, and so on alternately. Let them remain for a few hours, when break them up with the hand; put them in a nice cool place for 3 days, occasionally stirring and mashing them well, to extract from them as much juice as possible. Now measure the quantity of liquor without straining, and to each quart allow the above proportion of spices, &c. Put all into a stone jar, cover it up very closely, put it in a saucepan of boiling water, set it over the fire, and let it boil for 3 hours. Have ready a nice clean stewpan; turn into it the contents of the jar, and let the whole simmer very gently for ½ hour; pour it into a jug, where it should stand in a cool place till the next day; then pour it off into another jug, and strain it into very dry clean bottles, and do not squeeze the mushrooms. To each pint of ketchup add a few drops of brandy. Be careful not to shake the contents, but leave all the sediment behind in the jug; cork well, and either seal or rosin the cork, so as perfectly to exclude the air. When a very clear bright ketchup is wanted, the liquor must be strained through a very fine hair-sieve, or flannel bag, *after* it has been very gently poured off; if the operation is not successful, it must be repeated until you have quite a clear liquor. It should be examined occasionally, and if it is spoiling, should be reboiled with a few peppercorns. *Seasonable* from the beginning of September to the middle of October, when this ketchup should be made.

Note.—This flavouring ingredient, if genuine and well prepared, is one of the most useful store sauces to the experienced cook, and no trouble should be spared in its preparation. Double ketchup is made by reducing the liquor to half the quantity; for example, 1 quart must be boiled down to 1 pint. This goes farther than ordinary ketchup, as so little is required to flavour a good quantity of gravy. The sediment may also be bottled for immediate use, and will be found to answer for flavouring *thick* soups or gravies.

MUSHROOM POWDER (a valuable addition to Sauces and Gravies, when fresh Mushrooms are not obtainable).

Ingredients.—½ peck of large mushrooms, 2 onions, 12 cloves, ¼ oz. of pounded mace, 2 teaspoonfuls of white pepper. *Mode.*—Peel the mushrooms, wipe them perfectly free from grit and dirt, remove the black fur, and reject all those that are at all worm-eaten; put them into a stewpan with the above ingredients, but without water; shake them over a clear fire, till all the liquor is dried up, and be careful not to let them burn; arrange them on tins, and dry them in a slow oven; pound them to a fine powder, which put into small *dry* bottles; cork well, seal the corks, and keep it in a dry place. In using this powder, add it to the gravy just before serving, when it will merely require one boil-up. The flavour imparted by this means to the gravy, ought to be exceedingly good. *Seasonable.*—This should be made in September, or at the beginning of October.

Note.—If the bottles in which it is stored away are not perfectly dry, as, also, the mushroom powder, it will keep good but a very short time.

MUSHROOM SAUCE, very rich and good, to serve with Fowls or Rabbits.

Ingredients.—1 pint of mushroom-buttons, salt to taste, a little grated nutmeg, 1 blade of pounded mace, 1 pint of cream, 2 oz. of butter, flour to thicken. *Mode.*—Rub the buttons with a piece of flannel and salt, to take off the skin; cut off the stalks, and put them in a stewpan with the above ingredients, previously kneading together the butter and flour; boil the whole for about ten minutes, stirring all the time. Pour some of the sauce over the fowls, and the remainder serve in a tureen. *Time.*—10 minutes. *Average cost*, 2s. *Sufficient* to serve with a pair of fowls. *Seasonable* from August to October.

MUSHROOM SAUCE, Brown, to serve with Roast Meat, &c.

Ingredients.— ½ pint of button mushrooms, ½ pint of good beef gravy, 1 tablespoonful of mushroom ketchup (if at hand), thickening of butter and flour. *Mode.*—Put the gravy into a saucepan, thicken it, and stir over the fire until it boils. Prepare the mushrooms by cutting off the stalks, and wiping them free from grit and dirt; the large flap mushrooms cut into small pieces will answer for a brown sauce, when the buttons are not obtainable; put them into the gravy, and let them simmer very gently for about 10 minutes; then add the ketchup, and serve. *Time.*—Rather more than 10 minutes. *Seasonable* from August to October.

Note.—When fresh mushrooms are not obtainable, the powder may be used as a substitute for brown sauce.

MUSHROOM SAUCE, White, to serve with Boiled Fowls, Cutlets, &c.

Ingredients.—Rather more than ½ pint of button mushrooms, lemon-juice, and water, 1 oz. of butter, ½ pint of Béchamel, ¼ teaspoonful of pounded sugar. *Mode.*—Turn the mushrooms white by putting them into lemon-juice and water, having previously cut off the stalks and wiped them perfectly free from grit. Chop them, and put them in a stewpan with the butter. When the mushrooms are softened, add the Béchamel, and simmer for about 5 minutes; should they, however, not be done enough, allow rather more time. They should not boil longer than necessary, as they would then lose their colour and flavour. Rub the whole through a tammy, and serve very hot. After this, it should be warmed in a bain marie. *Time.*—Altogether ¼ hour. *Average cost*, 1s. *Seasonable* from August to October.

MUSHROOM SAUCE, White, to serve with Boiled Fowls, Cutlets, &c. (a more simple Method).

Ingredients.— ½ pint of melted butter, made with milk, ½ pint of button mushrooms, 1 dessertspoonful of mushroom ketchup, if at hand; cayenne and salt to taste. *Mode.*—Make the melted butter with milk, and add to it the mushrooms, which must be nicely cleaned, and free from grit, and the stalks cut off. Let them simmer gently for about 10 minutes, or until they are quite tender. Put in the seasoning and ketchup; let it just boil, when serve. *Time.*—Rather more than 10 minutes. *Average cost*, 8d. *Seasonable* from August to October.

MUSHROOMS, Baked (a Breakfast, Luncheon, or Supper Dish).

Ingredients.—16 to 20 mushroom-flaps, butter, pepper to taste. *Mode.*—For this mode of cooking, the mushroom-flaps are better than the buttons, and should not be too large. Cut off a portion of the stalk, peel the top, and wipe the mushrooms carefully with a piece of flannel and a little fine salt. Put them into a tin baking-dish, with a very small piece of butter placed on each mushroom; sprinkle over a little pepper, and let them bake for about 20 minutes, or longer should the mushrooms be very large. Have ready a *very hot* dish, pile the mushrooms high in the centre, pour the gravy round, and send them to table quickly, with very *hot* plates. *Time.*—20 minutes; large mushrooms, ½ hour. *Average cost,* 1*d.* each for large mushroom-flaps. *Sufficient* for 5 or 6 persons. *Seasonable.*—Meadow mushrooms in September and October; cultivated mushrooms may be had at any time.

MUSHROOMS, Broiled (a Breakfast, Luncheon, or Supper Dish).

BROILED MUSHROOMS.

Ingredients.—Mushroom-flaps, pepper and salt to taste, butter, lemon-juice. *Mode.*—Cleanse the mushrooms by wiping them with a piece of flannel and a little salt; cut off a portion of the stalk, and peel the tops; broil them over a clear fire, turning them once, and arrange them on a very hot dish. Put a small piece of butter on each mushroom, season with pepper and salt, and squeeze over them a few drops of lemon-juice. Place the dish before the fire, and when the butter is melted, serve very hot and quickly. Moderate-sized flaps are better suited to this mode of cooking than the buttons: the latter are better in stews. *Time.*—10 minutes for medium-sized mushrooms. *Average cost*, 1*d*. each for large mushrooms. *Sufficient.*—Allow 3 or 4 mushrooms to each person. *Seasonable.*—Meadow mushrooms in September and October; cultivated mushrooms may be had at any time.

MUSHROOMS, Dried.

Mode.—Wipe them clean, take away the brown part, and peel off the skin; lay them on sheets of paper to dry, in a cool oven, when they will shrivel considerably. Keep them in paper bags, which hang in a dry place. When wanted for use, put them into cold gravy, bring them gradually to simmer, and it will be found that they will regain nearly their usual size.

MUSHROOMS, Pickled.

Ingredients.—Sufficient vinegar to cover the mushrooms; to each quart of mushrooms, 2 blades of pounded mace, 1 oz. of ground pepper, salt to taste. *Mode.*—Choose some nice young button mushrooms for pickling, and rub off the skin with a piece of flannel and salt, and cut off the stalks; if very large, take out the red inside, and reject the black ones, as they are too old. Put them into a stewpan, sprinkle salt over them, with pounded mace and pepper in the above proportion; shake them well over a clear fire until the liquor flows, and keep them there until they are all dried up again; then add as much vinegar as will cover them; just let it simmer for 1 minute, and store it away in stone jars for use. When cold, tie down with bladder and keep in a dry place: they will remain good for a length of time, and are generally considered delicious. *Seasonable.*—-Make this the same time as ketchup, from the beginning of September to the middle of October.

MUSHROOMS, to Preserve.

Ingredients.—To each quart of mushrooms, allow 3 oz. butter, pepper and salt to taste, the juice of 1 lemon, clarified butter. *Mode.*—Peel the mushrooms, put them into cold water, with a little lemon-juice; take them out and *dry* them very carefully in a cloth. Put the butter into a stewpan capable of holding the mushrooms; when it is melted, add the mushrooms, lemon-juice, and a seasoning of pepper and salt; draw them down over a slow fire, and let them remain until their liquor is boiled away, and they have become quite dry, but be careful in not allowing them to stick to the bottom of the stewpan. When done, put them into pots, and pour over the top clarified butter. If wanted for immediate use, they will keep good a few days without being covered over. To re-warm them, put the mushrooms into a stewpan, strain the butter from them, and they will be ready for use. *Average cost*, 1*d.* each. *Seasonable.*—Meadow mushrooms in September and October; cultivated mushrooms may be had at any time.

MUSHROOMS, Stewed.

Ingredients.—1 pint mushroom-buttons, 3 oz. of fresh butter, white pepper and salt to taste, lemon-juice, 1 teaspoonful of flour, cream or milk, ¼ teaspoonful of grated nutmeg. *Mode.*—Cut off the ends of the stalks, and pare neatly a pint of mushroom-buttons; put them into a basin of water, with a little lemon juice, as they are done. When all are prepared, take them from the water with the hands, to avoid the sediment, and put them into a stewpan with the fresh butter, white pepper, salt, and the juice of ½ lemon; cover the pan closely, and let the mushrooms stew gently from 20 to 25 minutes; then thicken the butter with the above proportion of flour, add gradually sufficient cream, or cream and milk, to make the sauce of a proper consistency, and put in the grated nutmeg. If the mushrooms are not perfectly tender, stew them for 5 minutes longer, remove every particle of butter which may be floating on the top, and serve. *Time.*—½ hour. *Average cost*, from 9*d*. to 2*s*. per pint. *Sufficient* for 5 or 6 persons. *Seasonable*.—Meadow mushrooms in September and October.

MUSHROOMS, Stewed in Gravy.

Ingredients.—1 pint of mushroom-buttons, 1 pint of brown gravy, ¼ teaspoonful of grated nutmeg, cayenne and salt to taste. *Mode*.—Make a pint of brown gravy, cut nearly all the stalks away from the mushrooms and peel the tops; put them into a stewpan, with the gravy, and simmer them gently from 20 minutes to ½ hour. Add the nutmeg and a seasoning of cayenne and salt, and serve very hot. *Time*.—20 minutes to ½ hour. *Average cost*, 9*d*. to 2*s*. per pint. *Sufficient* for 5 or 6 persons. *Seasonable*.—Meadow mushrooms in September and October.

MUSTARD, How to Mix.

Ingredients.—Mustard, salt and water. *Mode*.—Mustard should be mixed with water that has been boiled and allowed to cool; hot water destroys its essential properties, and raw cold water might cause it to ferment. Put the mustard into a cup, with a small pinch of salt, and mix with it very gradually sufficient boiled water to make it drop from the spoon without being watery. Stir and mix well, and rub the lumps well down with the back of a spoon, as well-mixed mustard should be perfectly free from these. The mustard-pot should not be more than half-full, or rather less if it will not be used for a day or two, as it is so much better when it is freshly mixed.

MUSTARD, Indian, an excellent Relish to Bread and Butter, or any cold Meat.

Ingredients.—¼ lb. of the best mustard, ¼ lb. of flour, ½ oz. of salt, 4 shalots, 4 tablespoonfuls of vinegar, 4 tablespoonfuls of ketchup, ¼ bottle of anchovy sauce. *Mode*.—Put the mustard, flour, and salt into a basin, and make them into a stiff paste with boiling water. Boil the shalots with the vinegar, ketchup, and anchovy sauce, for 10 minutes, and pour the whole, *boiling,* over the mixture in the basin; stir well, and reduce it to a proper thickness; put it into a bottle, with a bruised shalot at the bottom, and store away for use. This makes an excellent relish, and if properly prepared will keep for years.

MUSTARD, Tartar.

Ingredients.—Horseradish vinegar, cayenne, ½ a teacupful of mustard. *Mode.*—Have ready sufficient horseradish vinegar to mix with the above proportion of mustard; put the mustard into a cup, with a slight seasoning of cayenne; mix it perfectly smooth with the vinegar, adding this a little at a time; rub down with the back of a spoon any lumps that may appear, and do not let it be too thin. Mustard may be flavoured in various ways, with Tarragon, shalot, celery, and many other vinegars, herbs, spices, &c.

MUTTON.

Almost every large city has a particular manner of cutting up, or, as it is called, dressing the carcase. In London this process is very simple, and as our butchers have found that much skewering back, doubling one part over another, or scoring the inner cuticle or fell, tends to spoil the meat and shorten the time it would otherwise keep, they avoid all such treatment entirely. The carcase when flayed (which operation is performed while yet warm), the sheep when hung up and the head removed, presents the profile shown in our cut; the small numerals indicating the parts or joints into which one-half of the animal is cut. After separating the hind from the fore quarters, with eleven ribs to the latter, the quarters are usually subdivided in the manner shown in the sketch, in which the several joints are defined by the intervening lines and figures. *Hind quarter*: No. 1, the leg; 2, the loin—the two, when cut in one piece, being called the saddle. *Fore quarter*: No. 3, the shoulder; 4 and 5 the neck; No. 5 being called, for distinction, the scrag, which is generally afterwards separated from 4, the lower and better joint; No. 6, the breast. The haunch of mutton, so often served at public dinners and special entertainments, comprises all the leg and so much of the loin, short of the ribs or lap, as is indicated on the upper part of the carcase by a dotted line.

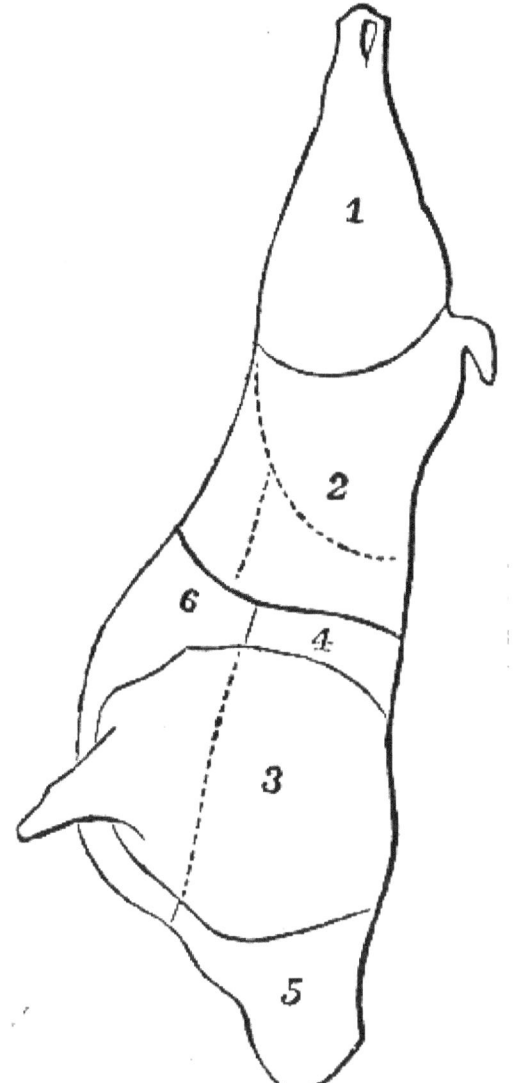

SIDE OF MUTTON, SHOWING THE SEVERAL JOINTS.

MUTTON, Baked Minced.

[Cold Meat Cookery.] *Ingredients.*—The remains of any joint of cold roast mutton, 1 or 2 onions, 1 bunch of savoury herbs, pepper and salt to taste, 2 blades of pounded mace or nutmeg, 1 teacupful of gravy, mashed potatoes. *Mode.*—Mince an onion rather fine, and fry it a light-brown colour; add the herbs and mutton, both of which should be also finely minced and well mixed; season with pepper and salt, and a little pounded mace or nutmeg, and moisten with the above proportion of gravy. Put a layer of mashed potatoes at the bottom of a dish, then the mutton, and then another layer of potatoes, and bake for about ½ hour. *Time.*—½ hour. *Average cost*, exclusive of the meat, 4d. *Seasonable* at any time.

Note.—If there should be a large quantity of meat, use 2 onions instead of 1.

MUTTON, Boiled Breast of, and Caper Sauce.

Ingredients.—Breast of mutton, bread-crumbs, 2 tablespoonfuls of minced savoury herbs (put a large proportion of parsley), pepper and salt to taste. *Mode.*—Cut off the superfluous fat; bone the meat; sprinkle over a layer of bread-crumbs, minced herbs, and seasoning; roll, and bind it up firmly. Boil *gently* for 2 hours, remove the tape, and serve with caper sauce, a little of which should be poured over the meat. *Time.*—2 hours. *Average cost*, 6*d.* per lb. *Sufficient* for 4 or 5 persons. *Seasonable* all the year.

MUTTON, an excellent way to cook a Breast of.

Ingredients.—Breast of mutton, 2 onions, salt and pepper to taste, flour, a bunch of savoury herbs, green peas. *Mode.*—Cut the mutton into pieces about 2 inches square, and let it be tolerably lean; put it into a stewpan, with a little fat or butter, and fry it of a nice brown; then dredge in a little flour, slice the onions, and put it with the herbs in the stewpan; pour in sufficient water *just* to cover the meat, and simmer the whole gently until the mutton is tender. Take out the meat, strain, and skim off all the fat from the gravy, and put both the meat and gravy back into the stewpan; add about a quart of young green peas, and let them boil gently until done. 2 or 3 slices of bacon added and stewed with the mutton give additional flavour; and, to insure the peas being a beautiful green colour, they may be boiled in water separately, and added to the stew at the moment of serving. *Time.*—2½ hours. *Average cost*, 6*d.* per lb. *Sufficient* for 4 or 5 persons. *Seasonable* from June to August.

MUTTON, Broiled, and Tomato Sauce.

[Cold Meat Cookery.] *Ingredients.*—A few slices of cold mutton, tomato sauce. *Mode.*—Cut some nice slices from a cold leg or shoulder of mutton; season them with pepper and salt, and broil over a clear fire. Make some tomato sauce, pour it over the mutton, and serve. This makes an excellent dish, and must be served very hot. *Time.*—About 5 minutes to broil the mutton. *Seasonable* in September and October, when tomatoes are plentiful and seasonable.

MUTTON BROTH, to Make.

Ingredients.—1 lb. of the scrag end of the neck of mutton, 1 onion, a bunch of sweet herbs, ½ turnip, 3 pints of water, pepper and salt to taste. *Mode.*—Put the mutton into a stewpan; pour over the water cold, and add the other ingredients. When it boils, skim it very carefully, cover the pan closely, and let it simmer very gently for an hour; strain it, let it cool, take off all the fat from the surface, and warm up as much as may be required, adding, if the patient be allowed to take it, a teaspoonful of minced parsley which has been previously scalded. Pearl barley or rice are very nice additions to mutton broth, and should be boiled as long as the other ingredients. When either of these is added, the broth must not be strained, but merely thoroughly skimmed. Plain mutton broth without seasoning is made by merely boiling the mutton, water, and salt together, straining it, letting the broth cool, skimming all the fat off, and warming up as much as is required. This preparation would be very tasteless and insipid, but likely to agree with very delicate stomachs, whereas the least addition of other ingredients would have the contrary effect. *Time.*—1 hour. *Average cost*, 7*d*. *Sufficient* to make from 1½ to 2 pints of broth. *Seasonable* at any time.

Note.—Veal broth may be made in the same manner; the knuckle of a leg or shoulder is the part usually used for this purpose. It is very good with the addition of the inferior joints of a fowl, or a few shank-bones.

MUTTON BROTH, to Make Quickly.

Ingredients.—1 or 2 chops from a neck of mutton, 1 pint of water, a small bunch of sweet herbs, ¼ of an onion, pepper and salt to taste. *Mode.*—Cut the meat into small pieces; put it into a saucepan with the bones, but no skin or fat; add the other ingredients; cover the saucepan, and bring the water quickly to boil. Take the lid off, and continue the rapid boiling for 20 minutes, skimming it well during the process; strain the broth into a basin; if there should be any fat left on the surface, remove it by laying a piece of thin paper on the top; the greasy particles will adhere to the paper, and so free the preparation from them. To an invalid nothing is more disagreeable than broth served with a quantity of fat floating on the top; to avoid this, it is always better to allow it to get thoroughly cool, the fat can then be so easily removed. *Time.*—20 minutes after the water boils. *Average cost,* 5*d.* *Sufficient* to make ½ pint of broth. *Seasonable* at any time.

MUTTON, Haunch of, to Carve.

A deep cut should, in the first place, be made quite down to the bone, across the knuckle-end of the joint, along the line 1 to 2. This will let the gravy escape; and then it should be carved, in not too thick slices, along the whole length of the haunch, in the direction of the line from 4 to 3.

HAUNCH OF MUTTON.

MUTTON, Leg of, to Carve.

This homely, but capital English joint, is almost invariably served at table as shown in the engraving. The carving of it is not very difficult: the knife should be carried sharply down in the direction of the line from 1 to 2, and slices taken from either side, as the guests may desire, some liking the knuckle-end, as well done, and others preferring the more underdone part. The fat should be sought near the line 3 to 4. Some connoisseurs are fond of having this joint dished with the under-side uppermost, so as to get at the finely-grained meat lying under that part of the joint, known as the Pope's eye; but this is an extravagant fashion, and one that will hardly find favour in the eyes of many economical British housewives and housekeepers.

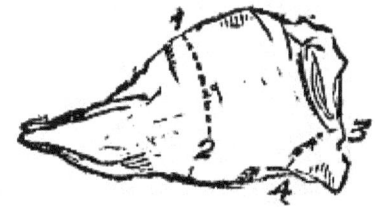

LEG OF MUTTON.

MUTTON, Loin of, to Carve.

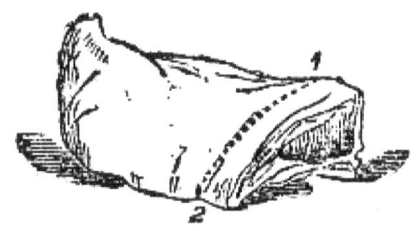

LOIN OF MUTTON.

There is one point in connection with carving a loin of mutton which includes every other; that is, that the joint should be thoroughly well jointed by the butcher before it is cooked. This knack of jointing requires practice and the proper tools; and no one but the butcher is supposed to have these. If the bones be not well jointed, the carving of a loin of mutton is not a gracious business; whereas, if that has been attended to, it is an easy and untroublesome task. The knife should be inserted at fig. 1, and after feeling your way between the bones, it should be carried sharply in the direction of the line 1 to 2. As there are some people who prefer the outside cut, while others do not like it, the question as to their choice of this should be asked.

MUTTON, Saddle of, to Carve.

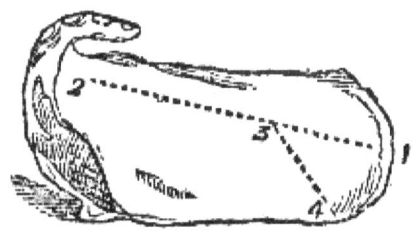

SADDLE OF MUTTON.

Although we have heard, at various intervals, growlings expressed at the inevitable "saddle of mutton" at the dinner-parties of our middle classes, yet we doubt whether any other joint is better liked, when it has been well hung and artistically cooked. There is a diversity of opinion respecting the mode of sending this joint to table; but it has only reference to whether or no there shall be any portion of the tail, or, if so, how many joints of the tail. Some trim the tail with a paper frill. The carving is not difficult: it is usually cut in the direction of the line from 2 to 1, quite down to the bones, in evenly-sliced pieces. A fashion, however, patronized by some, is to carve it obliquely, in the direction of the line from 4 to 3; in which case the joint would be turned round the other way, having the tail end on the right of the carver.

MUTTON, Shoulder of, to Carve.

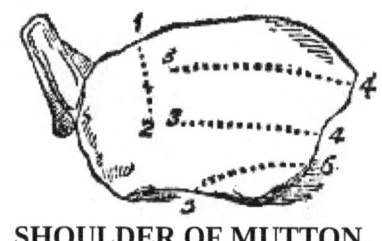

SHOULDER OF MUTTON.

This is a joint not difficult to carve. The knife should be drawn from the outer edge of the shoulder in the direction of the line from 1 to 2, until the bone of the shoulder is reached. As many slices as can be carved in this manner should be taken, and afterwards the meat lying on each side of the blade-bone should be served, by carving in the direction of 3 to 4 and 5 to 6. The uppermost side of the shoulder being now finished, the joint should be turned, and slices taken off along its whole length. There are some who prefer this under-side of the shoulder for its juicy flesh, although the grain of the meat is not so fine as that on the other side.

MUTTON CHOPS, Broiled.

Ingredients.—Loin of mutton, pepper and salt, a small piece of butter. *Mode.*—Cut the chops from a well-hung tender loin of mutton, remove a portion of the fat, and trim them into a nice shape; slightly beat and level them; place the gridiron over a bright clear fire, rub the bars with a little fat, and lay on the chops. Whilst broiling, frequently turn them, and in about 8 minutes they will be done. Season with pepper and salt, dish them on a very hot dish, rub a small piece of butter on each chop, and serve very hot and expeditiously. *Time.*—About 8 minutes. *Average cost*, 10d. per lb. *Sufficient.*—Allow 1 chop to each person. *Seasonable* at any time.

MUTTON-COLLOPS.

Ingredients.—A few slices of a cold leg or loin of mutton, salt and pepper to taste, 1 blade of pounded mace, 1 small bunch of savoury herbs minced very fine, 2 or 3 shalots, 2 or 3 oz. of butter, 1 dessertspoonful of flour, ½ pint of gravy, 1 tablespoonful of lemon-juice. *Mode.*—Cut some very thin slices from a leg or the chump end of a loin of mutton; sprinkle them with pepper, salt, pounded mace, minced savoury herbs, and minced shalot; fry them in butter, stir in a dessertspoonful of flour, add the gravy and lemon-juice, simmer very gently about 5 or 7 minutes, and serve immediately. *Time.*—5 to 7 minutes. *Average cost,* exclusive of the meat, 6*d*. *Seasonable* at any time.

MUTTON, Curried.

[Cold Meat Cookery.] *Ingredients.*—The remains of any joint of cold mutton, 2 onions, ¼ lb. of butter, 1 dessertspoonful of curry-powder, 1 dessertspoonful of flour, salt to taste, ¼ pint of stock or water. *Mode.*—Slice the onions in thin rings, and put them into a stewpan with the butter, and fry of a light brown; stir in the curry-powder, flour, and salt, and mix all together. Cut the meat into nice thin slices (if there is not sufficient to do this, it may be minced), and add it to the other ingredients; when well browned, add the stock or gravy, and stew gently for about ½ hour. Serve in a dish with a border of boiled rice, the same as for other curries. *Time.*—½ hour. *Average cost,* exclusive of the meat, 6*d*. *Seasonable* in winter.

MUTTON CUTLETS, with Mashed Potatoes.

Ingredients.—About 3 lbs. of the best end of the neck of mutton, salt and pepper to taste, mashed potatoes. *Mode.*—Procure a well-hung neck of mutton, saw off about 3 inches of the top of the bones, and cut the cutlets of a moderate thickness. Shape them by chopping off the thick part of the chine-bone; beat them flat with a cutlet-chopper, and scrape quite clean, a portion of the top of the bone. Broil them over a nice clear fire for about 7 or 8 minutes, and turn them frequently. Have ready some smoothly-mashed white potatoes; place these in the middle of the dish; when the cutlets are done, season with pepper and salt; arrange them round the potatoes, with the thick end of the cutlets downwards, and serve very hot and quickly. *Time.*—7 or 8 minutes. *Average cost,* for this quantity, 2*s*. 4*d*. *Sufficient* for 5 or 6 persons. *Seasonable* at any time.

MUTTON CUTLETS.

Note.—Cutlets may be served in various ways; with peas, tomatoes, onions, sauce piquant, &c.

MUTTON, Braised Fillet of, with French Beans.

Ingredients.—The chump end of a loin of mutton, buttered paper, French beans, a little glaze, 1 pint of gravy. *Mode.*—Roll up the mutton in a piece of buttered paper, roast it for 2 hours, and do not allow it to acquire the least colour. Have ready some French beans, boiled, and drained on a sieve; remove the paper from the mutton, glaze it; just heat up the beans in the gravy, and lay them on the dish with the meat over them. The remainder of the gravy may be strained, and sent to table in a tureen. *Time.*—2 hours. *Average cost*, 8½d. per lb. *Sufficient* for 4 or 5 persons. *Seasonable* at any time.

MUTTON, Haricot.

Ingredients.—4 lbs. of the middle or best end of the neck of mutton, 3 carrots, 3 turnips, 3 onions, pepper and salt to taste, 1 tablespoonful of ketchup or Harvey's sauce. *Mode.*—Trim off some of the fat, cut the mutton into rather thin chops, and put them into a frying-pan with the fat trimmings. Fry of a pale brown, but do not cook them enough for eating. Cut the carrots and turnips into dice, and the onions into slices, and slightly fry them in the same fat that the mutton was browned in, but do not allow them to take any colour. Now lay the mutton at the bottom of a stewpan, then the vegetables, and pour over them just sufficient boiling water to cover the whole. Give the boil, skim well, and then set the pan on the side of the fire to simmer gently until the meat is tender. Skim off every particle of fat, add a seasoning of pepper and salt, and a little ketchup, and serve. This dish is very much better if made the day before it is wanted for table, as the fat can be so much more easily removed when the gravy is cold. This should be particularly attended to, as it is apt to be rich and greasy if eaten the same day it is made. It should be served in rather a deep dish. *Time.*—2½ hours to simmer gently. *Average cost,* for this quantity, 3*s*. *Sufficient* for 6 or 7 persons. *Seasonable* at any time.

MUTTON, Haricot.

Ingredients.—Breast or scrag of mutton, flour, pepper, and salt to taste, 1 large onion, 3 cloves, a bunch of savoury herbs, 1 blade of mace, carrots and turnips, sugar. *Mode.*—Cut the mutton into square pieces, and fry them a nice colour; then dredge over them a little flour and a seasoning of pepper and salt. Put all into a stewpan, and moisten with boiling water, adding the onion, stuck with 3 cloves, the mace, and herbs. Simmer gently till the meat is done, skim off all the fat, and then add the carrots and turnips, which should be previously cut in dice and fried in a little sugar to colour them. Let the whole simmer again for 10 minutes; take out the onion and bunch of herbs, and serve. *Time.*—About 3 hours to simmer. *Average cost*, 6*d.* per lb. *Sufficient* for 4 or 5 persons. *Seasonable* at any time.

MUTTON, Haricot.

[Cold Meat Cookery.] *Ingredients.*—The remains of cold neck or loin of mutton, 2 oz. of butter, 3 onions, 1 dessertspoonful of flour, ½ pint of good gravy, pepper and salt to taste, 2 tablespoonfuls of port wine, 1 tablespoonful of mushroom ketchup, 2 carrots, 2 turnips, 1 head of celery. *Mode.*—Cut the cold mutton into moderate-sized chops, and take off the fat; slice the onions, and fry them with the chops, in a little butter, of a nice brown colour; stir in the flour, add the gravy, and let it stew gently nearly an hour. In the mean time boil the vegetables until *nearly* tender, slice them, and add them to the mutton about ¼ hour before it is to be served. Season with pepper and salt, add the ketchup and port wine, give one boil, and serve. *Time.*—1 hour. *Average cost*, exclusive of the cold meat, 6*d.* *Seasonable* at any time.

MUTTON, Hashed.

Ingredients.—The remains of cold roast shoulder or leg of mutton, 6 whole peppers, 6 whole allspice, a faggot of savoury herbs, ½ head of celery, 1 onion, 2 oz. of butter, flour. *Mode.*—Cut the meat in nice even slices from the bones, trimming off all superfluous fat and gristle; chop the bones and fragments of the joints, put them into a stewpan with the pepper, spice, herbs, and celery; cover with water, and simmer for 1 hour. Slice and fry the onion of a nice pale-brown colour, dredge in a little flour to make it thick, and add this to the bones, &c. Stew for ¼ hour, strain the gravy, and let it cool; then skim off every particle of fat, and put it, with the meat, into a stewpan. Flavour with ketchup, Harvey's sauce, tomato sauce, or any flavouring that may be preferred, and let the meat gradually warm through, but not boil, or it will harden. To hash meat properly, it should be laid in cold gravy, and only left on the fire just long enough to warm through. *Time.*—1½ hour to simmer the gravy. *Average cost*, exclusive of the meat, 4*d*. *Seasonable* at any time.

MUTTON, Roast Haunch of.

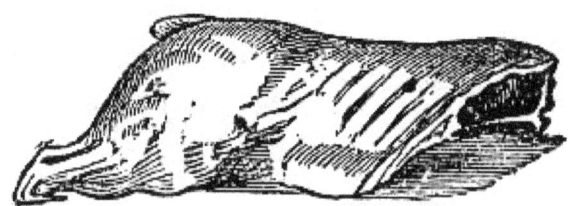

HAUNCH OF MUTTON.

Ingredients.—Haunch of mutton, a little salt, flour. *Mode.*—Let this joint hang as long as possible without becoming tainted, and while hanging dust flour over it, which keeps off the flies, and prevents the air from getting to it. If not well hung, the joint, when it comes to table, will do credit neither to the butcher nor the cook, as it will not be tender. Wash the outside well, lest it should have a bad flavour from keeping; then flour it and put it down to a nice brisk fire, at some distance, so that it may gradually warm through. Keep continually basting, and about ½ hour before it is served, draw it nearer to the fire to get nicely brown. Sprinkle a little fine salt over the meat, pour off the dripping, add a little boiling water slightly salted, and strain this over the joint. Place a paper ruche on the bone, and send red-currant jelly and gravy in a tureen to table with it. *Time.*—About 4 hours. *Average cost*, 10*d*. per lb. *Sufficient* for 8 to 10 persons. *Seasonable.*—In best season from September to March.

MUTTON, Boiled Leg of.

Ingredients.—Mutton, water, salt. *Mode.*—A leg of mutton for boiling should not hang too long, as it will not look a good colour when dressed. Cut off the shank-bone, trim the knuckle, and wash and wipe it very clean; plunge it into sufficient boiling water to cover it; let it boil up, then draw the saucepan to the side of the fire, where it should remain till the finger can be borne in the water. Then place it sufficiently near the fire, that the water may gently simmer, and be very careful that it does not boil fast, or the meat will be hard. Skim well, add a little salt, and in about 2¼ hours after the water begins to simmer, a moderate-sized leg of mutton will be done. Serve with carrots and mashed turnips, which may be boiled with the meat, and send caper sauce to table with it in a tureen. *Time.*—A moderate-sized leg of mutton of 9 lbs., 2¼ hours after the water boils; one of 12 lbs., 3 hours. *Average cost*, 8½d. per lb. *Sufficient.*—A moderate-sized leg of mutton for 6 or 8 persons. *Seasonable* nearly all the year, but not so good in June, July, and August.

Note.—When meat is liked very *thoroughly* cooked, allow more time than stated above. The liquor this joint was boiled in should be converted into soup.

MUTTON, Boned Leg of, Stuffed.

Ingredients.—A small leg of mutton, weighing 6 or 7 lbs., forcemeat, 2 shalots finely minced. *Mode.*—Make a forcemeat, to which add 2 finely-minced shalots. Bone the leg of mutton, without spoiling the skin, and cut off a great deal of the fat. Fill the hole up whence the bone was taken with the forcemeat, and sew it up underneath, to prevent its falling out. Bind and tie it up compactly, and roast it before a nice clear fire for about 2½ hours or rather longer; remove the tape and send it to table with a good gravy. It may be glazed or not, as preferred. *Time.*—2½ hours, or rather longer. *Average cost*, 4s. 8d. *Sufficient* for 6 or 7 persons. *Seasonable* at any time.

MUTTON, Braised Leg of.

Ingredients.—1 small leg of mutton, 4 carrots, 3 onions, 1 faggot of savoury herbs, a bunch of parsley, seasoning to taste of pepper and salt, a few slices of bacon, a few veal trimmings, ½ pint of gravy or water. *Mode.*—Line the bottom of a braising-pan with a few slices of bacon, put in the carrots, onions, herbs, parsley, and seasoning, and over these place the mutton. Cover the whole with a few more slices of bacon and the veal trimmings, pour in the gravy or water, and stew very *gently* for 4 hours. Strain the gravy, reduce it to a glaze over a sharp fire, glaze the mutton with it, and send it to table, placed on a dish of white haricot beans boiled tender, or garnished with glazed onions. *Time.*—4 hours. *Average cost*, 5s. *Sufficient* for 6 or 7 persons. *Seasonable* at any time.

MUTTON, Roast Leg of.

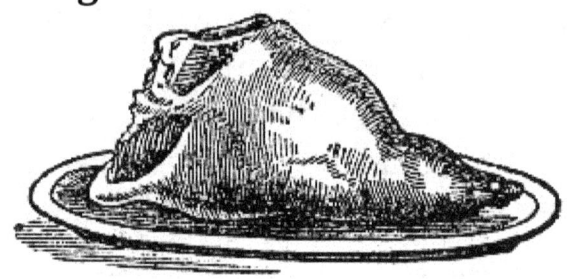

LEG OF MUTTON.

Ingredients.—Leg of mutton, a little salt. *Mode.*—As mutton, when freshly killed, is never tender, hang it almost as long as it will keep; flour it, and put it in a cool airy place for a few days, if the weather will permit. Wash off the flour, wipe it very dry, and cut off the shank-bone; put it down to a brisk clear fire, dredge with flour, and keep continually basting the whole time it is cooking. About 20 minutes before serving, draw it near the fire to get nicely brown; sprinkle over it a little salt, dish the meat, pour off the dripping, add some boiling water slightly salted, strain it over the joint, and serve. *Time.*—A leg of mutton weighing 10 lbs., about 2¼ or 2½ hours; one of 7 lbs., about 2 hours, or rather less. *Average cost*, 8½d. per lb. *Sufficient.*—A moderate-sized leg of mutton sufficient for 6 or 8 persons. *Seasonable* at any time, but not so good in June, July, and August.

MUTTON, Roast Loin of.

Ingredients.—Loin of mutton, a little salt. *Mode.*—Cut and trim off the superfluous fat, and see that the butcher joints the meat properly, as thereby much annoyance is saved to the carver, when it comes to table. Have ready a nice clear fire (it need not be a very wide large one), put down the meat, dredge with flour, and baste well until it is done. Make the gravy as for roast leg of mutton, and serve very hot. *Time.*—A loin of mutton weighing 6 lbs., 1½ hour, or rather longer. *Average cost*, 8½d, per lb. *Sufficient* for 4 or 5 persons. *Seasonable* at any time.

LOIN OF MUTTON.

MUTTON, Rolled loin of (very Excellent).

Ingredients.—About 6 lbs. of a loin of mutton, ½ teaspoonful of pepper, ¼ teaspoonful of pounded allspice, ¼ teaspoonful of mace, ¼ teaspoonful of nutmeg, 6 cloves, forcemeat, 1 glass of port wine, 2 tablespoonfuls of mushroom ketchup. *Mode.*—Hang the mutton till tender, bone it, and sprinkle over it pepper, mace, cloves, allspice, and nutmeg in the above proportion, all of which must be pounded very fine. Let it remain for a day, then make a forcemeat, cover the meat with it, and roll and bind it up firmly. Half bake it in a slow oven, let it grow cold, take off the fat, and put the gravy into a stewpan; flour the meat, put it in the gravy, and stew it till perfectly tender. Now take out the meat, unbind it, add to the gravy wine and ketchup as above, give one boil, and pour over the meat. Serve with red-currant jelly; and, if obtainable, a few mushrooms stewed for a few minutes in the gravy, will be found a great improvement. *Time.*—1½ hour to bake the meat, 1½ hour to stew gently. *Average cost*, 4*s.* 9*d.* *Sufficient* for 5 or 6 persons. *Seasonable* at any time.

Note.—This joint will be found very nice if rolled and stuffed, as here directed, and plainly roasted. It should be well basted, and served with a good gravy and currant jelly.

MUTTON, Boiled Neck of.

Ingredients.—4 lbs. of the middle, or best end of the neck of mutton; a little salt. *Mode.*—Trim off a portion of the fat, should there be too much, and if it is to look particularly nice, the chine-bone should be sawn down, the ribs stripped half-way down, and the ends of the bones chopped off; this is, however, not necessary. Put the meat into sufficient *boiling* water to cover it; when it boils, add a little salt and remove all the scum. Draw the saucepan to the side of the fire, and let the water get so cool that the finger may be borne in it; then simmer very *slowly* and gently until the meat is done, which will be in about 1½ hour, or rather more, reckoning from the time that it begins to simmer. Serve with turnips and caper sauce, and pour a little of it over the meat. The turnips should be boiled with the mutton; and when at hand, a few carrots will also be found an improvement. These, however, if very large and thick, must be cut into long thinnish pieces, or they will not be sufficiently done by the time the mutton is ready. Garnish the dish with carrots and turnips, placed alternately round the mutton. *Time.* —4 lbs. of the neck of mutton, about 1½ hour. *Average cost,* 8½d. per lb. *Sufficient* for 6 or 7 persons. *Seasonable* at any time.

MUTTON, Ragoût of Cold Neck of.

[COLD MEAT COOKERY.] *Ingredients.*—The remains of a cold neck or loin of mutton, 2 oz. of butter, a little flour, 2 onions sliced, ½ pint of water, 2 small carrots, 2 turnips, pepper and salt to taste. *Mode.*—Cut the mutton into small chops, and trim off the greater portion of the fat; put the butter into a stewpan, dredge in a little flour, add the sliced onions, and keep stirring till brown; then put in the meat. When this is quite brown, add the water, and the carrots and turnips, which should be cut into very thin slices; season with pepper and salt, and stew till quite tender, which will be in about ¾ hour. When in season, green peas may be substituted for the carrots and turnips: they should be piled in the centre of the dish, and the chops laid round. *Time.*—¾ hour. *Average cost,* exclusive of the meat, 4d. *Seasonable,* with peas, from June to August.

MUTTON, Roast Neck of.

Ingredients.—Neck of mutton; a little salt. *Mode.*—For roasting, choose the middle, or the best end, of the neck of mutton, and if there is a very large proportion of fat, trim off some of it, and save it for making into suet puddings, which will be found exceedingly good. Let the bones be cut short, and see that it is properly jointed before it is laid down to the fire, as they will be more easily separated when they come to table. Place the joint at a nice brisk fire, dredge it with flour, and keep continually basting until done. A few minutes before serving, draw it nearer the fire to acquire a nice colour, sprinkle over it a little salt, pour off the dripping, add a little boiling water slightly salted; strain this over the meat and serve. Red-currant jelly may be sent to table with it. *Time.*—4 lbs. of the neck of mutton, rather more than 1 hour. *Average cost,* 8½d. per lb. *Sufficient* for 4 or 6 persons. *Seasonable* at any time.

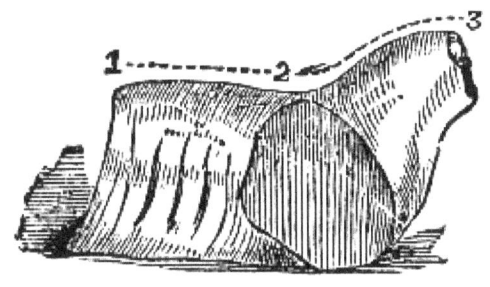

NECK OF MUTTON.
1-2. *Best end.*   2-3. *Scrag.*

MUTTON PIE.

[COLD MEAT COOKERY.] *Ingredients.*—The remains of a cold leg, loin, or neck of mutton, pepper and salt to taste, 2 blades of pounded mace, 1 dessertspoonful of chopped parsley, 1 teaspoonful of minced savoury herbs; when liked, a little minced onion or shalot; 3 or 4 potatoes, 1 teacupful of gravy; crust. *Mode.*—Cold mutton may be made into very good pies if well seasoned and mixed with a few herbs; if the leg is used, cut it into very thin slices; if the loin or neck, into thin cutlets. Place some at the bottom of the dish; season well with pepper, salt, mace, parsley, and herbs; then put a layer of potatoes sliced, then more mutton, and so on till the dish is full; add the gravy, cover with a crust, and bake for 1 hour. *Time.*—1 hour. *Seasonable* at any time.

Note.—The remains of an underdone leg of mutton may be converted into a very good family pudding, by cutting the meat into slices, and putting them into a basin lined with a suet crust. It should be seasoned well with pepper, salt, and minced shalot, covered with a crust, and boiled for about three hours.

MUTTON PIE.

Ingredients.—2 lbs. of the neck or loin of mutton, weighed after being boned; 2 kidneys, pepper and salt to taste, 2 teacupfuls of gravy or water, 2 tablespoonfuls of minced parsley; when liked, a little minced onion or shalot; puff crust. *Mode.*—Bone the mutton, and cut the meat into steaks all of the same thickness, and leave but very little fat. Cut up the kidneys, and arrange these with the meat neatly in a pie-dish; sprinkle over them the minced parsley and a seasoning of pepper and salt; pour in the gravy, and cover with a tolerably good puff crust. Bake for 1½ hour, or rather longer, should the pie be very large, and let the oven be rather brisk. A well-made suet crust may be used instead of puff crust, and will be found exceedingly good. *Time.*—1½ hour, or rather longer. *Average cost*, 2*s*. *Sufficient* for 5 or 6 persons. *Seasonable* at any time.

MUTTON PUDDING.

Ingredients.—About 2 lbs. of the chump end of the loin of mutton, weighed after being boned; pepper and salt to taste, suet crust made with milk, in the proportion of 6 oz. of suet to each pound of flour; a very small quantity of minced onion (this may be omitted when the flavour is not liked). *Mode.*—Cut the meat into rather thin slices, and season them with pepper and salt; line the pudding-dish with crust; lay in the meat, and nearly, but do not quite, fill it up with water; when the flavour is liked, add a small quantity of minced onion; cover with crust, and proceed in the same manner as directed in recipe for [rump steak and kidney pudding](). *Time.*—About 3 hours. *Average cost*, 1*s*. 9*d*. *Sufficient* for 6 persons. *Seasonable* all the year, but more suitable in winter.

MUTTON, Roast Saddle of.

Ingredients.—Saddle of mutton; a little salt. *Mode.*—To insure this joint being tender, let it hang for ten days or a fortnight, if the weather permits. Cut off the tail and flaps, and trim away every part that has not indisputable pretensions to be eaten, and have the skin taken off and skewered on again. Put it down to a bright, clear fire, and, when the joint has been cooking for an hour, remove the skin and dredge it with flour. It should not be placed too near the fire, as the fat should not be in the slightest degree burnt, but kept constantly basted, both before and after the skin is removed. Sprinkle some salt over the joint; make a little gravy in the dripping-pan; pour it over the meat, which send to table with a tureen of made gravy and red-currant jelly. *Time.*—A saddle of mutton weighing 10 lbs., 2½ hours; 14 lbs., 3¼ hours. When liked underdone, allow rather less time. *Average cost*, 10*d.* per lb. *Sufficient.*—A moderate-sized saddle of 10 lbs. for 7 or 8 persons. *Seasonable* all the year; not so good when lamb is in full season.

SADDLE OF MUTTON.

MUTTON, Roast Shoulder of.

Ingredients.—Shoulder of mutton; a little salt. *Mode.*—Put the joint down to a bright, clear fire; flour it well, and keep continually basting. About ¼ hour before serving, draw it near the fire, that the outside may acquire a nice brown colour, but not sufficiently near to blacken the fat. Sprinkle a little fine salt over the meat, empty the dripping-pan of its contents, pour in a little boiling water slightly salted, and strain this over the joint. Onion sauce, or stewed Spanish onions, are usually sent to table with this dish, and sometimes baked potatoes. *Time.*—A shoulder of mutton weighing 6 or 7 lbs., 1½ hour. *Average cost*, 8*d.* per lb. *Sufficient* for 5 or 6 persons. *Seasonable* at any time.

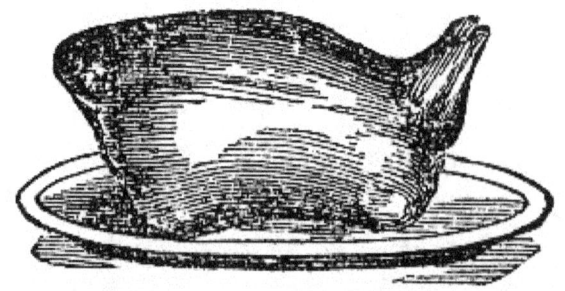

SHOULDER OF MUTTON.

Note.—Shoulder of mutton may be dressed in a variety of ways; boiled, and served with onion sauce; boned, and stuffed with a good veal forcemeat; or baked, with sliced potatoes in the dripping-pan.

MUTTON SOUP, Good.

Ingredients.—A neck of mutton about 5 or 6 lbs., 3 carrots, 3 turnips, 2 onions, a large bunch of sweet herbs, including parsley; salt and pepper to taste; a little sherry, if liked; 3 quarts of water. *Mode.*—Lay the ingredients in a covered pan before the fire, and let them remain there the whole day, stirring occasionally. The next day put the whole into a stewpan, and place it on a brisk fire. When it commences to boil, take the pan off the fire, and put it on one side to simmer until the meat is done. When ready for use, take out the meat, dish it up with carrots and turnips, and send it to table; strain the soup, let it cool, skim off all the fat, season and thicken it with a tablespoonful, or rather more, of arrowroot; flavour with a little sherry, simmer for 5 minutes, and serve. *Time.*—15 hours. *Average cost*, including the meat, 1*s.* 3*d.* per quart. *Seasonable* at any time. *Sufficient* for 8 persons.

NASTURTIUMS, Pickled (a very good Substitute for Capers).

Ingredients.—To each pint of vinegar, 1 oz. of salt, 6 peppercorns, nasturtiums. *Mode.*—Gather the nasturtium pods on a dry day, and wipe them clean with a cloth; put them in a dry glass bottle, with vinegar, salt, and pepper, in the above proportion. If you cannot find enough ripe to fill a bottle, cork up what you have got until you have some more fit; they may be added from day to day. Bung up the bottles, and seal or rosin the tops. They will be fit for use in 10 or 12 months; and the best way is to make them one season for the next. *Seasonable.*—Look for nasturtium-pods from the end of July to the end of August.

www.ingramcontent.com/pod-product-compliance
Lightning Source LLC
Chambersburg PA
CBHW081624100526
44590CB00021B/3595